Yeshua
of
Nazareth

spiritual
master

Yeshua of Nazareth

spiritual master

The Spirituality He
Lived and Taught

RICHARD W. CHILSON

SORIN BOOKS   Notre Dame, Indiana

International Standard Book Number: 1-893732-27-4

Cover and text design by Brian C. Conley

Printed and bound in the United States of America.

Library of Congress Cataloging-in-Publication Data
Chilson, Richard.
    Yeshua of Nazareth : the spirituality he lived and taught / Richard W. Chilson.
        p. cm.
    ISBN 1-893732-27-4 (pbk.)
1. Spiritual life--Christianity. I. Title.
    BV4501.3 .C48 2001
    232--dc21

                                        00-011332

For Trish and Scott
and all the other seekers

CONTENTS

INTRODUCTION

Sooner or later every spiritual seeker—Christian or non-Christian, religious believer or nonbeliever—owes it to himself or herself to take a serious look at the spiritual way of Yeshua of Nazareth, the way that he himself lived and preached before there were churches or even apostles.

Since the name "Jesus" is overly familiar to most people, in this book we will use his Hebrew name, "Yeshua." This will help to remind us that we are looking at him with a fresh eye, not concerned about the religion that claims him as its own, but rather at the teachings of the man before he was proclaimed the "Christ" and made the foundation of the western world. To pursue spiritual growth while ignoring the wisdom of this towering figure of western spirituality doesn't make sense. His "way" belongs side by side with the "ways" of all the other great spiritual teachers and traditions, however fashionable it may be to act otherwise.

After centuries in which it has become deeply entangled with western politics, culture, and religion, getting to the "way of Yeshua" can be difficult. It is, however, unquestioningly worth the effort.

The nonbeliever will recognize in Yeshua an earthly teacher like any other but one whose wisdom has become an acknowledged cornerstone of western civilization.

In Yeshua Jews will find a "wise man," a rabbi to be honored with other teachers of the law. A rather radical teacher, granted, but a rabbi nonetheless.

In Yeshua the Muslim will find an accepted precursor to Mohammed and to the full revelation of Islam—not the Savior, but a prophet of Allah.

For the Buddhist, Hindu, and Taoist, it means learning from a great western spiritual teacher without the burdens of secular history. Yeshua is a teacher that they will discover to have much in common with their own sages. His teachings might even help Easterners gain further insights into their own traditions.

Christians may have the hardest route to travel. For them it will be especially hard to get beyond centuries of theological formulation, religious practice, and a personal "been-there-done-that-and-didn't-much-care-for-the-experience" attitude. But it can be done.

Anyone, in fact, whatever his or her starting point, will find in the way of Yeshua, in the way he lived and died, in his sermons, and above all in his stories, something that will almost certainly speak to their souls at the most profound level, no matter what their personal spiritual history might be.

They will find that the way of Yeshua is at once shockingly simple and enormously demanding . . .

You shall love the Lord your God,
with all your mind,
your heart,
your strength.
And your neighbor as yourself.

In time, Yeshua of Nazareth—whose way this was and is—would become for many the Christ, the anointed one, the Messiah. In these pages, though, he remains the simple teacher available to all.

But be warned: in these pages Yeshua of Nazareth is not kept at arm's length. To understand his way, even if approached out of mere curiosity, you must become involved. There is no substitute for testing its value by doing it his way.

Chapter 1

A HUNGER FOR HAPPINESS

W hat are we looking for?
And why?

If life is a banquet, it has been said, then most poor
bastards are starving.
And surely we, the most overstuffed people in history, are
especially pathetic.
Beneath our material abundance lurks famine of a deeper
kind.
Are we sated?—oh, yes!
Satisfied?—no!

For what do we thirst? Hard to say.
Consider holidays when we were kids . . .
Once in particular;
I wanted something expensive and important:
I forget what.
But at the time I dreamed, lived, planned, ached:
it would change my life.

13

The great day's here!
  One after another my parents shower gifts
    beyond my expectations.
  With all these surely I won't get my desire . . .
  But the grand finale reveals it in all its glory!

Yet by afternoon the hunger for more,
  for something else, resumes gnawing at my heart.

  We consign these gifts to the attic of forgetfulness,
  but the experience remains vivid and familiar,
  renewed through each succeeding expectation,
  reinforced through each sinking realization
  that neither this time nor probably next
  will the golden grail bring true peace and serenity.

Know the feeling? Sure we do.
We've built an economy that plays
  and preys upon such childlike anticipation.
Nothing lasts!
Continuous consumption turns the wheel.
  It's broke?
  Not to worry, the new model is so much better;
  consider yourself lucky you're in the market.
Our world's one commandment: consume!

But beneath the thirst for the new and improved
  lies a deeper longing for something that lasts,

14

for a feeling of being satisfied,
for a contentment lasting beyond the moment,
for rest, tranquility, harmony, peace.

Is it all some cruel joke?
Is the ultimate tragedy to get what we want and know it's
        not enough?
Given conveniences and luxuries
    that would have stunned our grandparents,
    we remain restless, unfulfilled, mildly bored,
        unengaged,
    longing for what we already know will disappoint.

It's not some cosmic jest, some inherent defect in our
        wiring.
We have known times of satisfaction,
    fleeting moments which we immediately
    tried to hold and preserve.
We have seen sunsets whose reds send our blood singing.
At moments we hear a music deeper than silence,
    singing of heart's longing and soul's repose.
We have known the gift of love
    which unmasks the eternal in one dear person
    and fills the most dreary existence with sufficiency
        and meaning.

And yet we continue to seek meaning
    in a material world.

If we can't count it, it's worthless, useless, a mirage.
How can we hope to find what we cannot see and barely
      comprehend;
  what our science will not stoop to affirm?

Our quest is ephemeral, airy, spiritual.
  That's it!
We are in search of the spiritual even though we may not
      think so,
  or truly know what it means.

How do we know this?
Our ancestors affirm it.
From before written records
  we have looked beyond the horizons dreaming of
      what lies there
  whether at the boundaries of land and sky
  or at the gates of life itself.
Our lives are curiously incomplete, something's lacking;
we fail to grasp the entire meaning:
something lies just beyond
  the here of geography,
  the now of time.
This life exceeds our grasp
  and at least for the poet, "that's what heaven's for."

So enter consumer spirituality to complete what's lacking,
    to supply what we seek.
"Come on down to the used spirituality supermarket!"
So hawks the psychic barker:
"Fill your basket with exotic delights,
    with a metaphysics of lives past
    that exposes why this one is so out of joint.
Take a dash of meditation:
    a quick hit of peace and harmony."

Fortunately few are motivated enough to stick it out.
We sample each fad up to the point of real work
    when our disappointment in instant enlightenment
    is soon seduced by something new.
The mandala of the New Age:
    a hamster wheel, running round, round, round,
    going aground.

The dealer shills cheap goods, but our questions are sincere:
    What will make our lives complete?
    What provides meaning and significance?
    How do we live a full life? Is peace possible?

The spiritual is not susceptible to a quick and easy fix.
True spirituality involves not so much feeling good or
        fulfilled
    as being changed, transformed into something more.

It demands discipline, practice, patience,
  even death to our old self.
Above all a trust in grace,
  the unforeseen, the unexpected,
  the unexplained, the undeserved.

Chapter 2

WHAT ARE WE LOOKING FOR?

So what are we really looking for?
How can we hope to find it or even recognize it if we do,
  given it is immaterial, ephemeral, spiritual?
If we can't describe it directly, can we speak around it?
Language and words can point us
  beyond themselves, as our forebears knew.
When confronted with the unexplainable,
  the unknowable, the unspeakable,
  they responded with stories.
Within the heart of story lies the power to point
  across space and time,
  and pass along the invisible.

"If I could explain what it means I wouldn't have had to
    make the film,"
  director Stanley Kubrick scolded critics
  asking reasoning questions of his millennial myth
  2001—A Space Odyssey.

"A poem doesn't mean—it is!" claimed John Chiardi in
      defiance of utility;
"A rose is a rose is a rose" chimed Gertrude Stein, her
      nonsense sense-full.
Image, poem, myth
      gains our closest entry to the mystery and mastery
      of Being:
      rose, chant, and star child over all.

"The Island" is such an evocation, a beachhead upon the
      mystery—
      not our own story; this comes from Sufis, Allah's
      mystical lovers.
But like all truth it oversteps boundaries.
Attend the tale of the Island now:
      let it flesh out our longing, our quest.
It suggests
      who we are,
      where we come from
      where we are,
      what our horizons might be.

*Long ago a group of people had to move from their beautiful
island home and migrate to a quite ordinary and poor island.
Someday they would be able to return to their homeland, but
that day was hundreds of years in the future. And since the
thought of the life they had lived on their island made their existence on this present miserable island even more intolerable, the
islanders soon began to "forget" how good life had been before.*

After a while, the previous life became only a wonderful dream to their children and grandchildren. But the descendants still cherished the wonderful news that someday it would be possible to return, and so they preserved the great art of shipbuilding so that when that day finally arrived, all would be able to make the journey home.

As hundreds of years passed, though, the memory of home grew dimmer and dimmer. In fact, many now claimed that there had never been a homeland. The art of shipbuilding came to appear as so much useless knowledge and activity. And soon they even forgot how to build them.

But all was not lost. A few people preserved the dream and cherished it, passing it on from believer to believer. Since no one knew the art of shipbuilding any longer, the only hope for return to the island lay in swimming.

Finally these few dreamers who had preserved the old ideas announced that it was time to make the return to the homeland. Of course, most of the islanders by now did not even know about the homeland. They looked at the swimming instructors with amused curiosity, perhaps had a good laugh, and then went about their daily business again. The swimming instructors told the people about the beautiful island that was their real home. While most thought the instructors a little crazy, a few people here and there believed them. And these believers presented themselves for swimming lessons so that they might make the great journey.

Such a person would come up to a swimming instructor and say, "I want to learn how to swim."

21

"All right," the instructor would reply. "But what is this bushel of cabbages you're dragging behind you?"

"I will need them for food when I finally arrive in the homeland."

"But the foods of the homeland are infinitely more nourishing and delicious than cabbages, so there is no need to carry all of that with you."

"You don't understand; I need this cabbage for food. How can you expect me to voyage out into the unknown without any food supply?"

"But it will be impossible for you to swim dragging those cabbages along with you. They will tire you long before you reach home; then they will drag you under, and you will drown."

"Well, in that case, I'm afraid I can't go. Because although you call my cabbages a hindrance, I consider them absolutely necessary to my well-being and survival."

Since so many conversations with the swimming instructors ended like this, very few ever returned to the homeland.

Does this vibrate to our longing?
Does it give us a reason for our being?
Suggest a haven for our restlessness?
Does it lift a little the veil of unknowing?
Does it whisper what we've always suspected?

Chapter 3

SO WHAT IS A WAY?

What can we learn from "The Island"
   about our own life,
   about our dreams and desires,
   about the obstacles in our way?

What's the greatest use of life?
"The Island" suggests it is
to make a journey from this mundane existence
   to something wondrous and shining.

We were not put here to stay put, but to progress,
   to wander in wonder toward our true harbor.

Think this is all there is?
Then we sit content with cabbages,
   and we've lost not only who we were meant to be
   but who we are.

The story offers diagnosis to critique our now:
    Something's missing.
Otherwise why the search for new horizons,
    new aeons, new worlds to conquer?

The Buddha said:
    Existence is inadequate.
    Life is suffering.
We may have known nothing but cabbages, but we'll
    never be content.

Bad news leads to good:
Diagnosis gives way to *vision*:
    It was not ever so.
    We come from afar.
Our discontent arises from memory of the better.
Our instincts speak true; we were not meant for this dull
    shore.
A richer island was exiled from our lives but not from our
    hearts.

Vision carries wisdom,
    The idea of ships and shipbuilding
    (though we may never even see a canoe, let alone
        build one)
    excites our imagination, feeds our yearning.

Visions vary; Paradises differ; ours is not the same as all,
for some a tropical luxuriance,
for others green pastures.

Yeshua points to heaven,
Buddha to nirvana.
Not the same at all:
two fingers pointing.

But then they speak wisdom. The differences lessen.
The details are different; but the essence rings the same.
Consider the following insights:

Hatreds do not ever cease in this world
by hating, but by love;
this is an eternal truth . . .
Overcome anger by love,
overcome the evil by good.
Overcome the miser by giving,
overcome the liar by truth.

Why do you see the speck in your neighbor's eye
but do not notice the log in your own?
How can you say to your neighbor,
"Friend, let me take the speck out of your eye,"
when you do not see the log in your own?
First take the log out of your own eye,
then you will see clearly
to remove the speck from your neighbor's eye.

Two fingers pointing,
    one from East,
    one from West.
But only one moon lies beyond all fingers
    and all true fingers point home.

Wisdom reveals how we might take sail,
    navigate by the stars and attain port safely;
    it is common to all.

We're not Sufis, whose dream was baked in desert mirage,
yet our pastoral idyll is best reached by the same
    skill of ships and skein of sailing as aids the Bedouin.
We all wish to go down to the sea, and home.

Practice makes the airy actual, makes our goal achievable.
Swimming lessons will make real what is now but dream:
    to reach the farther shore.

May practice make perfect,
    so we could just go with the flow, but cabbages tie
        us down.
Obstacles are as essential to the story as the hope of
    paradise.

Even should we learn swimming from book lore alone,
    and laugh at the differences between cabbages and
        kings,
we will sink like a rock once we try on our own.

Only a masterful teacher can lure us into the awareness
    that our own favorite kinks may indeed be sulfurous;
    and spark us to leave them behind.

Someone walk with me,
    know me,
    talk to me,
    listen to me,
    and safeguard me
    from the many pitfalls any evolution entails!
Pulling up on my own bootstraps only throttles my feet.

Teacher, sponsor, guru, guide,
    when we are ready to learn to swim, they'll appear.
But realize, to need a teacher,
    implies we don't know the subject!
If we keep the mind of a student, a learner,
    and we don't walk away exasperated like many
        cabbage-huggers who know what they
        want but not what they need:
    we might just swim home.

Looking back over this story we've described the spiritual
        way.
A way to life as lived in the sunlight of wisdom.
A way to life by practice,
    guided through the obstacles
    by a spiritual friend,
    so that together we might benefit all.

So it was for the Sufi,
> or for anyone treading the footprints of time
> who like Gautama sets out from home in search of
>> the truth.

The Sufi, Gautama, Yeshua all walked the same way.
But each forged a different path.
A path has unique signposts and adventures.
> It speaks a definite language.
> It acknowledges a common heritage.
> It is aware of our cultural foibles.

The Way, common to all, remains the same.
Many the paths; one the Way.

We need a concrete expression of the way of our particular
> journey:
> we need a path.

So the question follows:
> which one?

Chapter 4

COME, FOLLOW ME

Always on the move, he passes from place to place.
We are on a way, a path,
   from where we have been,
   to where we are now,
   to what we shall become.

Yeshua's forebears made a journey from slavery to freedom:
   from Egypt to a promised land.
He would say with all Israelites,
   "My ancestors were wandering Arameans."
The Greek hero Odysseus wanders his way home from
         Troy,
   ever seeking, ever searching,
   ever adventuring, ever longing for home.
Some say once he arrived home
   the journey was so deeply ingrained
   he soon set off for other worlds,
   past the threshold of the sun.

Our own past honors pilgrims who came here longing for
      a new start,
    a new life, a new England, a New World.

And so we are now poised at the start of a new journey
    to realize our true self,
    to find our true home.

And into whatever occupies us breaks this wanderer,
    who commands we follow him.

    Passing along by the Sea of Galilee,
        Yeshua saw Simon and Andrew his brother casting nets
           in the sea;
        for they were fishermen.
    And he said,
        "Follow me and I will make you fishers of men."
    Immediately they left their nets and followed him.
    Going a little farther,
        he saw James the son of Zeb'edee and John his
           brother,
        who were in their boat mending the nets.
    Immediately he called them;
        they left their father Zeb'edee in the boat with the
           hired servants,
        and followed him.

"Follow me."
No greater introduction than that.
A hint of something better down the road.
An invitation to adventure.
An offer of a new purpose in life, hazy at best.
No money-back guarantees, no assurances,
No display of credentials as to why we should trust him.
Just that call breaking into our fishing.

That's often how it comes.
Out of the blue, yet curiously close to us,
    touching our deepest yearnings.
No time for careful consideration, and weighing the
       alternatives.
Just that dare to follow.

To follow where? Who knows.
No stated plan or goal. No destination.
Just the journey.

Houses may lure us to believe we have a lasting place here.
Yeshua knows better,

> *Foxes have holes, Birds have nests.*
> *Humanity has no place to lay its head.*

We know we are going to die, and with that comes our
       hunger for "life."

All sorts of things can delude us, convince us they will
       never fail.
But underneath lies the truth: All will fail.
Is there anything that lasts?

Abandon home and job, take to the road;
       and the uncertainty of life accompanies us always.
If spirituality involves living in the truth,
       then certainly the reality of our own situation
       is ever before us on the road.

Christian monks slept in their coffins to remind them
       everything passes.
Lulled by the conveniences of modern life
       we are tempted to put off the search.
Maybe it's not all that important.

"Follow me":
       we will not find what we seek standing around and
       waiting.

Yeshua calls us out of ourselves and our accustomed
       world.
Leave behind
       old thoughts,

old ways of life,
    routines of feeling and behaving!

Yeshua wakes us from complacency with a purpose, a
        task.
"I'll make you fishers of men."

Let the image resonate within.
What does it suggest?
Ride with the impression,
    feeling tones,
    emotions,
    connotations.
What does it evoke?

Give up on answers.
Stay with questions.
Wrestle Yeshua's stories.
Push them into different situations.

For one thing, it's not all about you.
Something bigger seems underway.
So much that passes today for spirituality
    is just navel-gazing, a fall into narcissism.
What's in it for me? But what if we are the problem all
        along?

Yeshua recruits in some higher cause, just what is unclear
    as yet.
He invites us to something surpassing our own selves
    to embrace all people.
He awakens us not only to our own dreams,
    but to humanity's hopes.
Yeshua gives us nothing just for ourselves.
"Share it or lose it," he will warn us.
Only a constant flow of giving gives grace in its fullness.
Whatever he calls us to do, we at least sense now
    it will go beyond us to embrace the world.

He calls us to follow and promises we will draw in others.
Some grand project seems underway.
    "Get on board, there's a job to be done."
Hear those words spoken to us,
    "I will make you fishers of men."
There is a gathering in, a luring to become part of
    something.
That's all he says, yet with what authority:
    with what bait he invites!
Men drop their lives to follow him.

What's the lure?
Sure, we hardly know him, at least in this original way.
But what beckons us to the task?
What attracts us to set out on this journey?

Now let's ask, who receives that invitation?
Fishermen.
>No special preparation,
>no training necessary.
Ordinary people.
Who is called? Whoever can hear the invitation.
Laborers here,
>but soon tax collectors, collaborators with the
>>Romans,
>parasites on their own people;
prostitutes, used for pleasure, then scorned by their
>abusers;
lepers, exiled from human community for fear of contagion;
but don't stop yet,
Roman centurions who ask for help,
the oppressor and enemy;
and foreign women who worship the wrong God;
and yes, even lawyers
and other upstanding members of the community,
>who sometimes turn away in sorrow and break his
>heart.

We hear his words today. They didn't die two thousand
>years ago.
They summon us now.
Are we prepared?
>No.
>But that doesn't seem to matter.

The only question is:
Will we follow?

Life is a journey,
the Koran tells us,
and that journey is toward God.

Chapter 5

THE GOD · PROBLEM

Yeshua's teaching in twenty words:

You shall love the Lord your God,
*   with all your mind,*
*   your heart,*
*   your strength.*
And your neighbor as yourself.

Nothing unusual or shocking.
Orthodox Jewish teaching, two thousand years old then,
Muslims can agree as well.
So what is it that makes such a simple command so
        difficult?

Love's not an issue.
Who would deny the gift of love?
Who would claim love is not the most important thing in
        life?

Could be a problem with "yourself."
If I loved you as I love myself, you'd be in pretty bad shape.
But that is something a spiritual path will work on.

If anything hangs us up it's that short little cough of a word,
    "God."

It would take lifetimes to unpack
    our associations,
    feelings,
    and opinions around that click in the throat.

Just who is God?
The man with the big book, keeping score?
A bogey man to scare little children?
A cipher? A crutch?
The first cause? The last refuge?
We all have some history with the First Being.

Maybe our god is too small.
If we think we can understand, know,
    comprehend God, we are far from the truth.
God is beyond all attempts to know or understand.
"Your ways are not my ways,"
God tells the prophet Isaiah:
"Look up at the heavens,
    my thoughts are as far from your thoughts
    as the earth from the stars."

Go outside tonight and gaze up at the sky,
    some of that light took thousands of light years
    to travel here so we might see it.

So removed are the thoughts and ways of God from our
        own ideas.
Too many gods fit snugly into our back pockets.
They tell us what we want to hear;
    they affirm our own prejudices and opinions.
They are not gods but idols.
God can never be made into our instrument,
God cannot be manipulated,
God is infinitely beyond us
    in every possible way,
    and then some.

Thomas Aquinas said whatever we might say about God,
    in truth we could equally deny.
Say that God is good and we stretch our concept of goodness
        so far beyond its breaking point that at times God
        seems evil.
One day at prayer in chapel Thomas experienced God
        directly.
He never wrote another word, his *Summa* remains two-
        thirds complete.
"It's all straw," was all he said.

To learn from Yeshua we must take care our projected
        images

do not distort his God into our own,
something too easily done.

Say that one little word "God"
and each person who hears it fills in the blank with
      personal experience.
Keep asking: Is this the God of Yeshua?
What am I importing into this picture?
How am I interpreting what Yeshua says?
Am I making God over into my own image?
That is what we do in fact.
    We form our idol from church, from our parents,
    and from our own experience.
But is this the God of Yeshua? Is this the God he asks us
    to love?

If we are going to start at the beginning,
    let's really begin at the start.
Open everything to question and investigation.
Set his teaching alongside our own experience.
Does it jive? Does it contradict?
Does it conflict with our dogma
    or better still, our lived experience?

Begin to fill in Yeshua's God.

Right away, we meet a challenge,
    the bugaboo of patriarchal domination.
Yeshua calls God "Father."

But take note!
Yeshua is not exclusive in his language.
He uses feminine images as well:
    the woman kneading bread,
    the matron searching the lost coin,
    the mother hen with her chicks.

But mostly God is "heavenly Father":
What does your mind see?
    Distant sky god,
    god of storm and thundercloud,
    Father mysterious.
For we never feel the intimate, bodily connection with
        Father,
    we do with mother.
We are mother's flesh and blood.
No doubting her relationship to us.
Fathers are more distant, their relationship more tenuous.
Is this not how we approach God? Can we even trust God
        is there?

God the warrior,
    builder and destroyer of civilizations,
He who will provide for his children; protect from all
        harm.

What other ideas and experiences do we import into God
    when we hear that word, "Father"?
Perhaps we should pause to look more closely at what
    Yeshua himself meant.

Chapter 6

OUR HEARTS
BELONG TO PAPA

Fatherhood is a role that is often wanting today.
Our own father may have been absent, distant, feared.
But this deficiency is not necessarily something to project
    onto Yeshua's God.
Let Yeshua draw his own picture:

>   Approach a friend at midnight and say,
>   "Friend, lend me three loaves,
>   for a friend of mine has come on a journey,
>   and I have nothing to set before him."
>   Your friend responds,
>   "Don't bother me;
>   the door is now shut, my children are in bed.
>   I can't get up and give you anything."
>   I say,
>   even though he will not get up and give you something
>   because he is your friend,
>   still because of your need, he will rise and give you what
>   you need.

I tell you,

> *Ask, and it will be given you;*
> *seek, and you will find;*
> *knock, and the door will be opened.*

For whoever asks receives,
and whoever seeks finds,
and whoever knocks will find the door opened.

What father, if his son asks for a fish,
> *will instead give him a serpent;*
> *or if he asks for an egg, will give him a scorpion?*
If you then, limited as you are,
> *know how to give your children good gifts,*
how much more will your heavenly Father
> *give good things to those who ask him!*

God nurtures,
God forgives,
God loves.

Yeshua affirms the tradition of patriarchy with a catch.
He doesn't really call God "Father," but "Abba,"
> a diminutive,
> an endearment,
> a child's intimacy.
No accurate translation exists.
Think "Papa," or "Daddy," and come close.

When we address the most high God
    whose name must never be mentioned,
    creator of all, liberator of our people,
    as "Daddy" something is bound to change.
The mystery does not diminish, but tenderness blooms.
The far-off becomes approachable, familiar, beloved.

> *Because we are children,*
> > *God has sent the Spirit of Yeshua into our hearts,*
> > *crying, "Abba! Daddy!"*
> *We are no longer slaves but children,*
> *and if a child then also an heir, through God.*

So Paul interprets Yeshua's victory.

We begin to see ourselves as we truly are, small
    defenseless children,
    reaching out to the One who called us into being and
    loves us ever.

Indeed this is the first thing we must experience—
    this nurturing, empowering free gift of love
    surrounding us,
    penetrating us,
    raising us up,
    calling us God's own.

Until we experience this Love
    we cannot take the next step along the Way of Yeshua.
Imagine we alone are lost, isolated,
    confused, solitary.
So counsels Julian of Norwich, a twelfth-century
        Christian mystic.
Know that God would forsake everything
    to search us out, embrace us
    and bring us to the very center of God's bosom.
Yeshua says as much by naming
God a shepherd,
    who foolishly goes forth
    leaving behind his entire flock
    to find the one who has wandered astray.
When he finds the lost one,
    he raises him upon his shoulders
    and carries him back to the others
    with much rejoicing.

It is but a short step to St. John's deduction that
    "God is love.
    And whoever loves lives in God
    and God in them."

So it shall be with us.
Let us call this God Love.
This is not to say that God loves.
More than that:
    God is Love; Love is God.

Yeshua shows us how this love reaches out to us
    and asks nothing more than that we return love.

Mother Teresa of Calcutta told her students
    to remain in the chapel praying until God's love
    filled them to the brim and overflowed.
Only then were they to go to the streets
    to approach the sick and outcast
    to share that love in ministry and care.
And when God's love diminished:
    leave whatever they were doing; they were of no use
        then!
    Return to the chapel and pray until love once more
        carried them out.

"Love God with all your being,
    mind,
    heart,
    body.
And love the other—whoever that other may be—
    as yourself."

That's the whole kit and caboodle.
Everything else is commentary.

Chapter 7

EMBRACE
LOVE'S RULE

Why change?
Because that's what it means to
trust in the Rule of Love:
   the center of Yeshua's mission, the vision he lives.
Indeed Yeshua so enfleshed the Rule of Love in his own life
   that his followers began to focus more and more
   on him as the key image for Love's Domain.
But in doing so
   they forget the necessity for all people
   to adopt this way of life.
We worship the image rather than do as he did.

Yeshua's original metaphor is the Kingdom of God,
   but for modern people that image carries all sorts of
      baggage
   that would hinder us in appreciating Yeshua's true
      message.

Better to trust in Love's Domain,
    Love's Dominion,
    Love's Rule.
And when we see this image
    remember we still speak of God's Kingdom
    where the God who is Love rules.

Yet "Kingdom" misleads us,
misleads us into thinking this is a place.
Already the disciple Matthew, when writing his gospel,
    feeling uncomfortable using "God," substituted
        "heaven."
That led us to put Love's Domain far off and far away.

But Yeshua's teaching is not "pie in the sky when we die."
Yeshua teaches a career for our present life with our current
    affairs.

    Love's Domain is not for some future time;
        You can't point to the sign of its coming.
    Love's Domain is not some special spot;
        You can't point to the place of its coming.
    Love's Domain is already among you, here, now.

Yes, it is true; there is a "not-yet" trait to Love's Dominion.
Few of us manage to trust love completely
    and live our present lives under its guidance.

We must hope
in the power of Love to transform us
and trust that the work of being re-made in Love's
image
will continue somehow beyond our present life.

But that does not change the present fact:
The moment to act is now, truly the only time available.
And whether we do it completely or haphazardly,
any converting touch of love is bound to change us
and the world we inhabit.

Let's focus our attention and efforts upon this new reality,
this vision of truth.
Experience it: begin to taste it,
then give in to it
so that we might leaven the world with this new way
of living.

We are the gateway by which this Rule of Love enters our
world.
Our trust in Love's Power enables Love to influence
not only ourselves but all we meet.

We encounter the Dominion of Love through Yeshua's
parables.
These short stories, examples, and metaphors drawn
from ordinary life,
catch us, bring us up short,
cause us to open our eyes and minds to a new way of
seeing.

Yeshua does not speak directly of Love's Domain,
    not because he wants to be difficult,
    but because it is so different from our current sense of
        reality.
How can he describe a reality we experience only fleetingly?
So he selects common aspects of our experience,
    sometimes turns them upside down,
    or stretches them beyond their bounds,
    to offer a glimpse of Love's Rule.
He demands a new way of seeing;
    questioning our basic sense of what is real.
Parables can suggest possibilities without having to spell
        out details.

Consider *Alice in Wonderland* as a spiritual book.
Children still connect to the truth;
    one reason they sometimes frighten adults:
    children see the truth and at times blurt it out
        embarrassingly.
Alice falls down a rabbit hole, or through a looking glass
    and enters an upside-down world.
She finds herself painting white roses red so the Queen
        won't shout,
    "Off with their heads!"
We must play along with all sorts of crazy adult games to
        survive.

After a while the child grows up and becomes an adult
>who has mastered the games and learned to hide the
>>truth.
Quite soon we have forgotten altogether
>that the red roses are indeed but paint.

Yeshua's parables could be seen as just such a mirror
>or rabbit hole leading not to some upside-down crazy
>>land,
>but back to sanity and reality.
They provide ways out of a wonderland neither wonderful
>nor life-giving.

Consider parables as windows into a new reality.
They afford us an opportunity to peer through
>into a new way of seeing,
>thinking, and living.
And since they offer us a strange new world,
>let's take the time needed to adjust our eyes and mind.
They may be short and pithy, but it takes a lifetime to
>digest them.
>Take the time.
>Return to them again and again.
>There is more than one way to peel a parable.
No stale school of philosophy here.
No schoolmaster teaching us rules of conduct.
They free our mind, give wing to our fancy.

Enter them at your own risk from every possible angle,
    at least one viewpoint for each person or object in the
        tale.
Meditate upon them.
    St. Benedict suggests ruminating on Scripture
    as a cow chews on her cud.
Keep them in heart; dare rewrite them.
    Change the scene; alter the characters.
    Play! Imagine!
Then come back to the original and discover what has
        appeared
    and what was there all along.

Chapter 8

WAKE UP! CHANGE YOUR LIFE!

His first words sound a wake-up call:
  "Change your ways and trust in Love's Dominion."
No sleeping allowed.
Notice that in the gospels, where the disciples represent us,
  snoring prevails.

Ten bridesmaids took their lamps and went to meet
  the bridegroom.
  Five were foolish, five wise.
When the foolish took their lamps, they took no oil
  with them;
  but the wise took flasks of oil with their lamps.
As the bridegroom was delayed, all of them became
  drowsy and slept.
At midnight, a shout,
  "Look! Here is the bridegroom! Come out to
  meet him."
Then the maids got up and trimmed their lamps.

The foolish said to the wise,

"Give us some of your oil, for our lamps are going out."

But the wise replied,

"No! there will not be enough for you and for us;

you had better go to the dealers and buy some for yourselves."

And while they went to buy it, the bridegroom came.

Those who were ready went with him into the wedding banquet;

and the door was shut.

Later the other bridesmaids returned, saying,

"Lord, lord, open to us."

But he replied,

"Truly I tell you, I do not know you."

Keep awake therefore,

for you know neither the day nor the hour.

When will God enter our life? How will we meet God?

Only God knows.

But we've already heard the messenger.

If we don't want to be caught napping when it happens,

we must stay alert!

"Buddha" means "The Awakened One,"

and while Yeshua has a slightly different thrust to the spiritual path,

he too demands presence to the here and now.

He leaves his disciples behind to go off into the wilderness
        to pray.
Cut to its core, prayer is "practice of the presence of God,"
        and meditative forms usher us into this holy moment.
Almost every spirituality advises meditation:
        a basic tool for growth and development.
The eastern "Jesus Prayer" and the western "Cloud of
        Unknowing"
        are but two examples of Christian models.
Meditation gently changes our focus from "me" to "us":
        a necessary shift of focus.

Watch therefore,
        for you do not know on what day your Lord is coming.
But know this,
        that if the householder had known in what part of the
                night
        the thief was coming,
he would have watched
        and would not have let his house be broken into.
Therefore you also must be ready;
        for God is coming at an hour you do not expect.

Imagine sitting in the middle of the house.
We know the thief is coming,
        but have no clue where he will enter or when.
Keep a tense watch: we tire and fall asleep.
Keep too slack a watch: sleep's inevitable.

Balance between tension and relaxation.
Use Yeshua's image to find the space.

Alert but at rest.
Simply aware of whatever happens.
Acknowledge all, sounds, thoughts, feelings, sensations.
Then let them go.
Return to the simple watchfulness.
Whenever we stray,
simply return to awareness: no blame, no shame.

So simple a thing, we're tempted to fix it,
    improve it,
and we make a mess of it.
In fact, we're probably doing it right
    if we aren't too uptight or too lazy.
Only we can judge it. Only we can find it.
Trust; practice being alive to the moment!

Yeshua is an alarm, disrupting our comfortable ways of
        thinking and living.
No salve for our ruts and routines.
    "You have heads. Use them!"
There's no mystery
    to why they hang him out to dry after three years at
    most.

"Change your ways!"

How? Return to the basic commandment.

Love God
with all your mind,
with all your heart,
with all your soul,
with all your might.
And your neighbor as yourself.

Here's a beginning of transformation.

To love God, I must change my mind.

Many of the things I believe in have no part in Love's
Domain.

Examples? Try fear, worry, anxiety, judgment.

Realities that make the world go round.

Try leading a worry-free hour and find out addiction's
power.

Love's Dominion often resembles a world through a
looking-glass.

Everything's reversed.

Left is right. Up is down.

As for the change of mind involved in loving our neighbor,
switch from "I" to "we" as the universe's hub.

Easier said than done; I naturally look out for "number
one."

59

Change of heart is the shift to love.
It begins at home. Start by letting God's infinite love sink in.
That love searched me out in so many ways.
Yeshua irrupts into our lives. No invitation necessary.
No waiting until we are ready.
Into the midst of our fishing, he calls us to journey with him.
On the road we shall learn the depth,

the power, the riches of God's love for us.
God can't help loving. It's who God is: Love.
And love cannot be abstract.
God loves the beloved, the spot where each of us stands.

Want to learn to love?
First, learn to be loved.
Drop surprise. Forget the modesty of unworthiness.
Love is already hopelessly, helplessly head-over-heels
        for us.
Only when we surrender to Love's transforming power
        are we ready to love in return, both God and neighbor.

Last, let's change our actions.
No need for complicated ethical tomes.
Look to the traditions.
Judeo-Christian Commandments:
        love God
                don't settle for a lesser god
                take time out to just be
        honor father and mother,

> don't steal,
> don't commit adultery,
> don't kill,
> don't lie,
> don't try to take what is our neighbor's.

The same themes echo in Buddhism:

> don't kill,
> don't steal,
> don't lie,
> don't have illicit sex,
> avoid intoxicating substances.

It doesn't take a spiritual master to point the way.
But it makes no sense to follow a spiritual teacher

> if we are not prepared to begin living a kinder, gentler way.

Consider the obvious first. We know who we hurt.
Most likely, those we love.
We can't stop it easily,

> but we can begin to ask forgiveness, and seek ways
> to make amends.

But what of those who hurt me?
No matter what they do;

> it helps to realize they just want the same things we do.

Have compassion first on ourselves,

> and we'll find an abundance for others.

Chapter 9

FARMING
LOVE'S WAY

Pay attention!
A sower went out to sow.
As he sowed, some seeds fell along the path,
*   and the birds came and devoured them.*
Some fell on the rock;
*   as it grew up, it withered away, for lack of moisture.*
Other seeds fell upon thorns,
*   and the thorns grew up and choked them.*
Other seeds fell on good soil and brought forth grain,
*   growing up, increasing and yielding*
*   a hundred fold, sixty, thirty fold.*

Unfortunately we are unfamiliar with
    the original jumping-off place of many parables.
We aren't farmers.
And even if we are, we are not the farmers of Yeshua's day.

So we should not be surprised if Yeshua's farmer strikes
        us as strange.

No preparation of the land,
    no digging out rocks,
    erecting scarecrows to frighten off birds,
    no tearing up of weeds.
Just scattering seed. A profligate farmer.

Feel the freedom and letting go of the fling.
No cautious conservation here.
Extravagant pitching rather—
    along the roadside,
    among weeds,
    onto rocky ground,
    as well as the fertile field.
Earthly farmers know the cost of seed: it's not cheap.
They husband their resources, make every seed count.
This guy casts it to the wind.
Not for him
    careful plowing; soil preparation,
    followed by conscious planting a couple seeds every
        six inches.
Let seed carelessly rain down where it will.

Foolhardy? You bet!
But take another look at the worldly farmer.
No real guarantees here either in spite of caution and
        concern.
Birds still come and mock the scarecrow.

Weeds sneak back in.
And when all is done, if the sun and rain cooperate,
    what do we have? A decent crop. That's all.
Whereas Love's farmer reaps thirty, sixty, a hundredfold.
A wealthy glut, compared to a just return.
Some seed was lost, but the harvest overflows.
Here is a primary characteristic of Love's Domain.

We feel we live in a world of scarcity.
If we don't watch out, we could be left without enough.
How else explain how Americans can
    use over two-thirds of the world's goods,
    while being only one-third of its people?
There's just not enough to go around.
We have to act this way and look out for ourselves.
This overarching concern
    colors and shapes our entire life and our community
        as well.

But what if this is not true?
What if in reality there is not only enough but a
        super-abundance?
How might that change our thinking and acting?
This is hard to fathom.

Matthew explains that seed is the "Word of God";
    we may read instead "Love's Domain."

Love's Dominion then is cast generously upon the world.
But some are unable to receive it:
> we provide rocky ground, or weeds spring up and
> choke it off.
Despite all, the seed continues to be cast forth.
Could the problem be us?
How do we prevent Love's Domain from reaching us?

Where have we found it strewn?
Nature?
> At the seashore before the infinite.
> In the majesty of mountains.
> The brisk air of fall as leaves blush.
> The resurrection of spring.
Human relationships?
> Children say the darndest things.
> The mystery of our spouse.
> Friends and neighbors of different cultures and
> experiences.
Where have we found the Word of Love cast upon our
> world?
What hinders us from allowing that Word to take root
> there and flourish?

Don't fence Yeshua in. This parable contains the universal.
His fellow Jews would be upset
> that God's Word was not given to them exclusively.
It was their holy treasure,

carefully handed down from generation to generation.
Today some Christians would be scandalized to think the
    Word of God
  was not solely in their hands.
People must hear the Word through the right channels,
  in the right contexts.

But if the seed is the Word of God
    it is scattered to the four corners of the earth,
    suffers all the various mishaps that may occur,
    and still goes on,
    thirty, sixty, a hundredfold.
Find the Word in the Scriptures.
Whose Scriptures?
The parable hints in every Scripture;
    Jewish, Christian, Muslim, yes,
    but Hindu and Buddhist also,
    plus the wisdom of Native Americans.
Let's not narrow our sights,
    but expand until we feel we might lose
    ourselves in all the words, people, and things
    which broadcast Love's Word.

Read the parable another way.
Become a farmer.
What do we have to sow?
    Time?
    Talent?

Money?
Our life?
How do we go about this?
Do we carefully prepare the ground?
Drop a seed every six inches?
Put up scarecrows?
Spend hot afternoons weeding?
Worry the weather?

Now shift over into Yeshua's farmer.
Take the seed in hand.
Feel the potential bounty.
Sense the rich promise held. Feel the seed in your hand.
Now cast it to the winds.
Taste the generosity in this scattering gesture.
Act it out with your body,
experience the letting go, the surrender.

The seed is scattered.
What do we do now?
Worldly farmers will fret it into fruition.
Yeshua's farmer has already let go.
Too late to take back that generous, reckless action.
There's nothing we can do now but sit back and relax.
We've lost all control over the crop.
We've resigned ourselves to the trust that all will be well.

There's that word again: trust.

Yeshua asks us to rely on the Rule of Love.

Hundredfold harvests. Surrender of worry.

Are there ways the story helps us see occasions in our
own life

where we believe scarcity rules but in truth abundance
abounds?

Chapter 10

HOW DOES LOVE'S GARDEN GROW?

Love's Domain is as if
> *you should scatter seed upon the ground,*
> *then sleep and rise night and day,*
> *and the seed sprouts and grows,*
> *you know not how.*

The earth produces of itself,
> *first the blade,*
> *then the ear,*
> *then the full grain in the ear.*

But when the grain is ripe,
> *at once you put in the sickle, because harvest is*
> *here.*

How small and insignificant seed is compared with the fruit it bears!

The beginnings of this new way of living will be very small, seemingly insignificant, yet results are forthcoming.

Nothing can be done to help it along.
Once we have received the seed, we need only trust it will
      mature.
We can neither aid nor guide it.
We do not know how our spiritual life is working and
      progressing.
We are still in the first moments of acceptance.
Trust in God, sit back, and allow the germ to come to
      harvest!

A hard lesson for Americans.
We are so used to doing something. We want to be in
      charge.
We want to make sure the process proceeds well.

Trust or faith is the one thing required.
If we find ourselves trying to guide or force the process,
      though, we must not despair.
That too is part of the work: coming to know ourselves.
As we make mistakes and recognize them, simply revert
      to pure trust.
We may discover something about our manner of living
      which can lead us toward deeper trust and surrender
      as we move upon this new way.

Say we decide to practice meditation to help us come to
      know ourselves

and to quiet us sufficiently to allow God into our life
and to become aware of God's workings there.
Tradition suggests twenty minutes twice a day
as most beneficial for the beginner.
If that is good, we reason, then two hours a day would be
better.
We wish to help the process along.
But we are really forcing the process,
which could cause all sorts of problems.
Extensive meditation may open us to issues in our psyche
we are not yet able to face.
It may uncover waves of fear or terror.
Or we may commit ourselves
to a practice we are incapable of honoring:
a common and serious pitfall in spiritual discipline.
We are inviting failure.
We are the worst enemy we will encounter on this journey.
The worst temptations come disguised as doing
something better.
For now we have decided to trust in the reality of Love's
Dominion.
Renew this faith daily through a simple prayer.
Ask Papa for trust.
No more is needed or even desirable.

Love's Domain is like
>   *someone who sowed good seed in a field.*
While people slept, the enemy came,
>   *sowed weeds among the wheat, and went away.*
So when the plants came up and bore grain,
>   *then the weeds appeared also.*
The servants asked,
>   *"Did you not sow good seed in your field?*
>   *How then has it weeds?"*
The sower said, "An enemy has done this."
The servants replied, "Then do you want us to go and
>   *gather them?"*

"No; for gathering the weeds you may root
>   *up the wheat as well.*
Let both grow together until the harvest;
then I will tell the reapers,
'Gather the weeds first and bind them in bundles to be
>   *burned,*
>   *but gather the wheat into my barn.'"*

We may convince ourselves
we have a clue to the Rule of Love.
In truth we do not.
The only thing we can do is,
>   let go.

We distrust the advice to do nothing and be receptive.
It rubs against our very grain. Nature and nurture makes
      us "do-ers."
Our native philosophy is pragmatism. "We can do it," we
      tell ourselves.
But in Love's Dominion we assume a new definition
    where we will be known not for what we do,
    but for who we are:
    God's beloved children pure and simple.
We are becoming inhabitants of Love's Domain
    so we must let Love take charge.
Our only task (important and crucial)
    is to allow the process to occur
    and affirm our trust in what takes place.
Love will naturally bring to fulfillment what was sown in us.

As seed first begins to sprout, it is hard to tell
    what's wheat, what's weed.
As industrious and good people, we want to tend the garden.
    Go out there and pull up the weeds!
    Give the wheat a chance!
But if we go weeding we are bound to pull up wheat
    while leaving some weeds.
Stay out of the way! Let God do the work!
This is the major toil of Yeshua's way.

So in our life, consider relationships to people, food, things.
Is this good for my spiritual growth?
Is this an impediment to my spiritual growth?

Forget this fretting and worrying for now!
Just keep asking Love for help and guidance.
Continue inviting Love in and go through the day.
Growing in the Spirit means growth in insight and wisdom
            as well,
as the journey comes to fruition we will be able to discern
            the weeds.
There is time for all that—at harvest.
For now, do what is for now.

There we have it: three parables about seed.
Like seed, they do not surrender their meaning at once.
Nor do they simply mean one thing.

Play with them, toss them back and forth in your mind,
        take on different characters,
                not just the farmer, become the seed too,
                the hungry birds, yes, even the weeds.
What does each tell us? How does each connect to our life?
        Can these stories illuminate actual events and issues?
        Reveal our efforts to control what is happening?
No hurry. It's still a long time, hopefully, till harvest.

Chapter 11

MUSTARD, BIRDS, LEAVEN AND LOAVES

Love's Domain is like a grain of mustard seed
which someone took and sowed in a field;
it may be the smallest of all seeds,
but, once grown, it is the greatest of shrubs
and puts forth large branches,
so the birds of the air can make nests in its shade.

Chances are we've never seen a mustard plant.
Since this is a story of Love's Domain,
we are tempted to envision a great tree, to dignify so
noble a reality.

But we miss the parable's point.
Love's Dominion is not a noble oak whose branches
spread out
to embrace the earth and reach up to join earth with
heaven.
We are thrown off by his last phrase:

how the birds of the air will come and make nests in
its branches.

Yeshua's original audience would get the irony.
They knew a mustard plant is hardly a tree,
    rather a fairly large and rather ugly shrub.
That last word carries the image's humor.
The idea of birds nesting there is almost absurd,
        somewhat daft.
Picture the "birds of the air," a grand lofty phrase,
        nesting in a large shrub.

What does mustard reveal about Love's Domain?
As mustard brings out food's flavor,
so Love's Domain spices life.
Love's Domain adds a new dimension to life;
    we do not have to abandon who we are
    or what we do for something else.
It flavors our ordinary reality.
The Rule of Love contributes a depth and zest
    missing in our accustomed experience.

The common, humble image of the mustard seed
    also hints where we might look for Love's Domain.

Consider everyday things.
    Don't limit this vision to certain peak experiences.

Love's Domain is present here and now
in the ordinary moments.
Many searching for the spiritual look for the extra-ordinary:
mountain peaks, vast vistas.
Certainly God's breath is there,
but don't exclude God from the common:
the greater portion of our lives.
Mountain peaks do not suggest the whole of Yeshua's
Way.

Seeking them may distract us from the real work.

Asked about special spiritual gifts,
such as levitation, mystic raptures, and visions,
Teresa of Avila replied:
"I would rather have a sister
able to scrub the convent floors in charity and love."
Philip Neri, reputed to levitate regularly
during religious services,
once sighed as he left the altar,
"Anyone who prays for special gifts
does not know what they're doing."
The extraordinary, while part of the Way of Yeshua,
also distracts from the true work
found in the everyday moments and places.

One more thing about mustard bushes:
once it invades our land it takes over;
it is almost impossible to get rid of, a nuisance.

Again an insight into this Domain of Love.
The love we feel for that special someone is an experience
     of God
        inasmuch as it is true love rather than puppy love or
           simply lust.
Such a love turns us upside down, threatens to drive us
     crazy.
It consumes, invades, dominates,
Watch out: give Love's Domain an inch and it will take a
     mile!

> *What's the Domain of Love like?*
> > *It's like leaven that a woman took*
> > *and hid in three measures of flour, till it was all*
> > > *leavened.*

Like mustard and seed another common image:
     a woman at work kneading dough.
A feminine image: God's Domain rises above, transcends
     gender.
And the image is homey and useful,
     like mustard, enhancing life.

Also like mustard, leaven is worthless in itself.
But it is essential to make the dough rise.

These exotic images for us were quite familiar to Yeshua's
     audience.
He draws from the realm of everyday peasant experience.

Reminding us that in looking for Love's Domain,
we should search first into ordinary daily life.
Consider what we would naturally overlook.
Simple exchanges of daily life:
    a smile on a passerby,
    a chance meeting with a friend,
    children at play,
    a cat with a ball.
Where does this hidden Domain peek out at us?
What raises our life and our world up?

And how might we join in kneading the leaven into life?
Love's Domain is not something we simply receive,
    but something received for others.
    If we do not pass it on, we are unable to enjoy its
        presence ourselves.
    That woman bakes not only for herself but for her
        family.

We are going to see more and more the importance of
    giving.
In the Greater Buddhist tradition
    giving is the first step on the way to enlightenment.
When Buddhists meditate, they begin each session
    by dedicating the fruits of that meditation
    to lighten the suffering of all beings.

They meditate not for themselves,
    not so that they can achieve something,
but to help all beings.
If we try to keep the fruits to ourselves, tradition claims,
    we forfeit all gains.
Give away these fruits and they last forever.

Most Westerners scoff.
Could that be why many never make any real progress?
If we are trying to learn how to make bread,
    it seems wise to follow directions.

Give away the fruits, and we enjoy the fruits of everyone
      else.
Keep them for ourselves; we shut down and lose all.

To practice leavening the loaf, don't look to the big things;
    consider the small opportunities.
    A kind word for the harried clerk or tollbooth guard.
    Let that driver in ahead.
    Leave little unexpected gifts for friends who will never
      know the donor.
    Give a brother or sister a break.

Crazy?
    Sure.

What does it cost?
    Not much.
What does it pay?
    We are leavening the loaf of Love.

Chapter 12

THE SEARCH IS MUTUAL

Love's Dominion is like treasure hidden in a field,
which a man found and covered up;
then in his joy he goes, sells all he has, and buys
that field.

Buried treasure: how many dreams has that idea
powered?
So great a find that when discovered,
all else pales into insignificance!
All that matters is to have this treasure.

Don't import "religious" ideas into this story.
Consider the possibility that it's not about "sacrifice" or
surrendering to God.
Yeshua is calling upon a very altruistic emotion:
greed.
Here's something we've just got to possess.

When have we encountered such "I've got to have it"
    situations?
We've all had them. They aren't reserved for the elite.
Lots of folks have had mystical moments.
We may not talk about them for fear of embarrassment,
    but God is generous with God's gifts.
Love's Domain is everywhere—the leaven in the loaf.
Consider special relationships:
    falling in love when we would do anything
    to have that person love us back.
What about the birth of children? Our feelings for our kids?

Use the treasure image to remember other experiences of
    finding something
    worth everything we own.
As these reflections come into awareness
    ask if this is not what it is like
    to be under the sway of Love's Domain?

Again, Love's Dominion is like a merchant searching out
        fine pearls,
    who, on finding one pearl of great value,
    went and sold all that he had and bought it.

On a quick reading the parable of the merchant
    merely repeats the buried treasure.
Only the names and objects have been changed.

Again there is a finding and the finder goes off to sell all
    to purchase the jewel.
But read closely! God's in the details.
Something has changed between the treasure and the pearl.
Can you spot the difference?

What part does Love's Domain play in each story?
There, it's treasure buried in a field.
Here, it's a merchant in search of fine pearls.
What does this say about God or Love?

The merchant story tells us we are not alone on this journey.
God is seeking us. And Love will go to any lengths to find
       and own us.
Papa does not wait around for us to come to Him.
God is not indifferent, withdrawn.
Love plunges into the world in search of the beloved,
    the pearl of great price.
Love is head over heels in God with us,
    and can't wait for the eventual meeting.
The prophet Mohammed said,
    "For every step we take toward God,
    God takes a thousand steps toward us."

And if God is the merchant, we are the pearl.
Do we see ourselves this way? Chances are we don't.
The world is not great at building up self-esteem.

Consider the pearl two ways:
First, it is a precious jewel. Rare and valued.
The oyster labors years to form it. It is difficult to find.
Divers risk their lives to harvest pearls.

Now take a more objective look at the pearl.
A piece of grit covered in spit.
At center is a grain of sand which, once inside the oyster's
        shell,
    becomes an irritant.
The oyster secretes the pearly substance to smooth the
        sand's edges.
Chances are we view ourselves this way:
    A piece of grit covered with spit. Nothing special.

But even if, in my own eyes, I am nothing,
in the merchant's eyes I am worth the world.
And that merchant will do whatever is necessary to
        possess me.
It is almost impossible to obtain a true image of ourselves.
We are so self-absorbed we are unable to see impartially.

If we open ourselves to others and ask how they see us
    we may move toward a more balanced view.
And to accept how God sees us helps most.
We encounter Someone willing to sacrifice for us, just as
    we are.

So how does Love's Domain come into this world?
Through following Love's will.
Can we come to trust that Love has our proper interests
         at heart?
Can we trust Love to care for us?

Do not answer that question quickly.
The path upon which Love may lead us is often quite far
      from the way we believe we should go.
The relationship Yeshua calls us into with Love will not be
      easy.
Teresa of Avila once complained to her God,
      "If this is the way you treat your friends,
      no wonder you have so few."
If we want a hint of where the path leads consider the last
      beatitude:

Happy are you when they slander you, persecute you,
      do all manner of things against you because
            of me.
Yours is the dominion of Love.

Is this the only way to the fullness of life we thirst for?
Many have answered "yes."
Yeshua encourages us to bring everything to Love.
Ask for whatever we want and need.

"Your will be done" balances the equation.
Ask for what we need, but surrender the final decision to
     Love.
What is Love's will for me? The great question.
Love, who created us, has a better idea of who we are
    and who we are meant to become
    than we do.

"Your will be done" can easily become the central action
    of every spirituality.
Islam puts it at the very core calling itself the "Way of
    Surrender."
It is here in Yeshua.
Other traditions offer the same teaching,
    leading us out of ourselves into a higher will.
Practice meditation, and we are confronted with our self will.
    It's boring. Nothing's happening. We're wasting time!
The manifestation of self will is part of the process.
As we come to know it, we learn to tame it.
We are beginning to follow a higher will
    with the entire creation's best interests at heart.
Do we trust enough to surrender to this higher power?
    This is the essence of spiritual work.
If we do not stumble upon the tension
    between ourselves and Love
    we are not working the path properly.
Chances are we identify Love's will with our own.
    A great deception.

No one is spared the contest.
Yeshua endures the same confrontation
at the end of his life in the garden.

Then Yeshua accompanied the disciples to a place
called Gethsemane;
he said, "Sit here while I go over there to pray."
He took Peter and the two sons of Zebedee,
and began to be upset and agitated.
Then he said to them,
"I am very upset, even to death;
stay here, and watch with me."
Going a little farther, threw himself on the ground and
prayed,
"My Father, if it is possible, let this cup pass me by;
yet not what I want but what you want."
When he came to the disciples he found them sleeping;
and said to Peter,
"So, could you not watch with me one hour?
Stay awake and pray you not be put to trial;
the spirit indeed is willing, but the flesh is weak."
He went away for the second time and prayed,
"My Father, if this cannot pass unless I drink it,
your will be done."
Again he came and found them asleep, for they were
exhausted.

Leaving them again, he went away and prayed a third time,
saying the same words.
Then he came to the disciples and said to them,
 "Are you still sleeping and taking your rest?
 See, the hour is here,
 and the Son of Man is betrayed into the hands of sinners.
 Get up, let us be going. See, my betrayer is here."

In all the various exercises we perform on this path, the bottom line is:
 are we are allowing Love's will to guide us?
How do we know something is Love's will?
Whatever happens to us is Love's will.
Love's horizons are infinitely broader than our own.
Love promises no rose garden.
How can we hope for an easier outcome than Yeshua endured?
The question remains which is the way to a richer, fuller, happier life?
 Our way? We know where that has led us.
Why not trust Love's way now?

Chapter 13

TEACH US TO PRAY

How do we move closer to this Domain of Love
glimpsed in the parables?
A key practice is prayer.
Prayer establishes a relationship between Love and us.
We actually approach Love and reveal ourselves to Love.
Love in turn reveals itself to us.

And we come to know one another.

Prayer is the way we relate to God or Love. So how do we
pray?

When you pray,
go into your room, shut the door
and pray to your Papa who is in secret;
and your Papa who sees in secret will reward you.
And in praying
do not heap up empty phrases as people do;
for they think they will be heard for their many
words.

Do not be like them, for your Papa knows what you
need before you ask.
Pray like this:
Papa,
May your name be revered.
Your will be done,
On earth as in your Domain.
Give us this day our daily bread;
And forgive us our sins,
As we also have forgiven those who sin against us;
And lead us not into temptation,
But deliver us from evil.

Prayer is a withdrawing from the outside
so that we might become attentive within.
What is secret within us? What is our spirit like?
We do not know what it looks like. But it gives us life.
When we pray, we withdraw into that secret place of the
spirit
to commune with God.

There's a practical application as well, especially for
beginners.
Allow the environment to lead to prayer.
Pick out a small area of the house as a place of prayer.
Erect an altar there: a small table is all that's needed.
Place some flowers, a picture we associate with Love.
Light a candle, burn incense to hallow the sacred space.

Experiment: discover what leads to the secret space within,
Use the objects as doors to prayer.
Pray in nature, at the beach, in the woods, on a mountain,
    in a garden.
Search out those places and things that lift us toward God;
    use them as aids in prayer.

Keep prayer simple.
    No use flattering God.
    Be natural. Use simple words.
    Trust that God knows us and cares for us.
Otherwise paraphernalia replaces prayer.

Don't rely too much on words.
When we are in Love, it is enough simply to be in the
    Beloved's presence.
Words may be necessary at first as we get acquainted,
    but let them subside as the relationship grows;
    it is good, it is enough, just to be together.

No need to put on airs. No need to impress.
Don't try to pretend to be someone else. Love knows us
    already.
God loves us already.
Be ourselves.
    And be persistent!

In a certain city a judge neither feared God nor
humanity;
and a widow in that city kept coming to him, saying,
"You've got to help me."
For a while he refused; but then he thought,
"Though I neither fear God nor humanity,
yet because this widow bothers me, I will support
her,
or she will wear me out by her continual demand."

It's a Warner Brothers' cartoon:
An arrogant judge hounded by a little widow.
Her entire life depends on her case,
    so she must devote all her attention and energy to it.
Finally she breaks through the judge's armor.
He doesn't deal with her because her cause is just,
    or because she has softened his heart.
He just wants to be left alone.

If even this narrow and arrogant judge gives in,
how much more is Papa going to listen to us
    when we bring him our life?
Do we dare do this?
Start in a small way: learn to trust what Yeshua teaches.
If it doesn't work look elsewhere for a teacher.
But take the first step of approaching Papa and ask for
      what's needed.

Prayer is a relationship between two persons.
We have seen how Yeshua describes God.
But what role should we take as we enter into this prayer
        relationship?
If God is Papa then are we not like little children?

> *I thank you, Papa, Lord of heaven and earth,*
> *because you have hidden these things from the wise*
>   *and the intelligent*
>   *and have revealed them to infants;*
> *yes, Papa, for such was your gracious will.*

Disciples are infants: neither wise nor intelligent.
Such a teaching is unlikely to please those in power.
They have everything to lose.
It is bound to appeal primarily to those who have nothing
        to lose,
        everything to gain.
The peasants of Yeshua's day, oppressed by the Roman
        empire
        and Jewish authorities who collaborated with
        Romans,
        formed an ideal audience for his teaching.

This raises a problem for most of us.
We are—in many ways—on the inside of the power
        structure
        rather than outside.

How are we to appropriate this teaching?
Yeshua's teaching is addressed to the poor, the outcast,
> the lame, the dead.
Does this mean we have no part of such teaching?

> *People were bringing little children to him*
> > *in order that he might touch them;*
> > *and the disciples spoke sternly to them.*
> *When Yeshua saw this, he was indignant and said to them,*
> > *"Let the little children come to me; do not stop them;*
> *Love's Dominion belongs to just such as these.*
> *I tell you, if you do not receive Love's Domain as a little child*
> > *you will never enter it."*
> *And he took them up in his arms, laid his hands on them, and*
> > *blessed them.*

In Yeshua's culture children were not the cuddly creatures
> we see them as.
A child was fairly useless
> unless it lived to support its parents in their old age.
> Many did not.
We must guard against reading our sentiments into this text.
Children are on the same level as lepers, the poor;
> they are lower than women in worth.
The disciples reflect their culture's prejudice when they
> try to protect Yeshua.

But Love's Domain belongs to the neglected and outcast.
And Yeshua adds, if we want a part of this Domain
    we must become like little children.
How are grown-ups to become like little children?

Francis of Assisi, one of Yeshua's greatest disciples,
    attempted to take Yeshua's teaching at face value.
He came from a rich family.
At the beginning of his journey along the path of Yeshua
    he stood in the public square of Assisi and removed
        all his clothing.
He did what little children do.
He was entering his spiritual life as naked
    as he entered this world.
We need not, dare not follow Francis too closely.
But there are ways in which we too can become like little
      children:
    we can put off the masks we wear in the public forum
    and in innocence approach the Way of Yeshua.

Two types of people can make this journey.
First are the poor in spirit—
    the poor, sick, alienated, rejected, persecuted,
      ignored by society.
Yeshua talks specifically to such people.
For example, a woman is not yet an equal member of
    human society.

Woman's journey of liberation to righteous equality with
    males
    is still incomplete everywhere today.
Such discrimination is our passport onto this spiritual way.

The second group wants to follow Yeshua, but is not
    marginalized.
For these he offers the possibility of becoming like little
    children.
Again this metaphor describes what cannot be laid out in
    detail.
Francis responded to it
    not with words but with his body and life.
He continued to respond this way throughout the journey,
    and becomes a model of Yeshua's teaching.

So what might it mean for us to become again a little child?
What kind of mind and spirit is needed?
What of our adult self do we have to put in abeyance?

It may be impossible to answer the question at this point.
Make it a practice to observe little children.
Notice their spontaneity, enthusiasm, lack of pretense.

It's not a question of becoming childish, but childlike.
Many spiritual paths describe a second childhood,
    a return to a time of innocence,
        but with the wisdom of the experienced.

Carry the question on the journey.
Other teachings will help us discover
    how to become childlike.
The circumstances of our own personal journey will
        reveal
    how it may be necessary to become a child.
Indeed part of the Way of Yeshua lies
    in recapturing that childhood spirit lost to adults.

Are not two sparrows sold for a penny?
And not one of them will fall to the ground without
        your Papa's will.
But even the hairs of your head are all numbered.
Fear not, therefore; you are of more value than many
        sparrows.

Chapter 14

THE MIRACLE OF THANKSGIVING

Want to move toward Love's Domain?
Simple.
Practice giving thanks.

Doesn't seem like much: as trivial as grace at meals.
This is the origin of such a prayer.
Don't make it trivial. Use it as a real practice. Let's put
ourselves behind it.
Not an automatic response,
but a genuine moment to stop and recognize all is gift.
It can transform our life.

When we realize that everything is ultimately a gift from Love
we experience gratitude.
That act of thanksgiving makes available to us
the abundance of Love's Domain.

Only one story about Yeshua,
> besides his death,
> is present in all four gospel accounts.

Its frequency marks its importance.

Further, Paul recounts a variant story:
> the earliest witness to an action of Yeshua.

> *For I received from the Lord what I also handed on to you,*
> *that the Lord Jesus on the night when he was betrayed*
>> *took a loaf of bread,*
>> *and when he had given thanks,*
>> *he broke it and said,*
>>> *"This is my body that is for you.*
>>> *Do this in remembrance of me."*
> *In the same way he took the cup also, after supper, saying,*
>> *"This cup is the new covenant in my blood.*
>> *Do this, as often as you drink it, in remembrance of me."*
> *For as often as you eat this bread and drink the cup,*
>> *you proclaim the Lord's death until he comes.*

Yes, this is the supper
> Yeshua shared with his disciples the night before he
>> died.

It has become the Christian eucharist.

But the passage of Yeshua's teachings from Eastern to
> Western culture
> obscures the story's fundamental elements.

104

Western philosophy focused upon the elements of the meal:
    bread and wine.
A Jew, such as Yeshua, considered the important
        elements
    not the nouns (the things),
    but rather the verbs (the actions).
What are the actions here?
    He took,
    He blessed,
    He broke,
    He gave (not present here but implied).
Of these four actions blessing or giving thanks is central.
Eucharist is Greek for "Thanksgiving."
Let's consider another thanksgiving story.

At evening, the disciples approached him and said,
    "This is a lonely place, and the day is now over;
    send the crowds away to go into the villages
    to buy food for themselves."
Yeshua said,
    "They need not go away; you give them something to eat."
They said,
    "We have only five loaves and two fish here."
And he said,
    "Bring them here to me."
Then he ordered the crowds to sit down on the grass;
    and taking the five loaves and the two fish
    he looked up to heaven, and blessed,

and broke
and gave the loaves to the disciples,
    and the disciples gave them to the crowds.
All ate and were satisfied.
Afterward they gathered twelve baskets full of the pieces left
    over.
There were about five thousand people.

We could regard this story as a miracle: Yeshua
        multiplies the bread and fish.
But the story itself does not indicate it is a miracle.
In miracle stories the crowd gapes in astonishment
    at the wonders Yeshua has performed. Not here.

How about a more natural solution?
Suppose some of these people had actually brought food
        with them?
Through Yeshua's act of generosity with his and the
        disciples' food,
    others might be encouraged to share openly so that
        all can eat.
Perhaps so. The story itself says nothing.

Mark and Matthew tell the story twice in their gospels.
Here is their second version:

Then Yeshua called his disciples to him and said,
> *"I have compassion on the crowd,*
> *because they have been with me now three days,*
> *and have nothing to eat;*
> *and I am unwilling to send them away hungry,*
> *lest they faint on the way."*

And the disciples said to him,
> *"Where are we to get bread enough in the desert*
> *to feed so great a crowd?"*

And Yeshua said to them, "How many loaves have you?"
They said, "Seven, and a few small fish."
And commanding the crowd to sit down on the ground,
> *he took the seven loaves and the fish,*
> *and having given thanks*
> *he broke them*
> *and gave them to the disciples,*
>> *and the disciples gave them to the crowds.*

And they all ate and were satisfied;
and they took up seven baskets full of the broken pieces left over.
Those who ate were four thousand.

In the first account the disciples approach Yeshua with
     their concern.
   It is natural enough. They fear people will grow hungry.
   When that happens, they will turn surly,
     being far from food and refreshment.
The disciples are planning ahead; they are helping the
     teacher.

Obviously he is concerned about higher things
 and does not notice hunger approaching.
It would be good to warn him.

Have we not had such ideas?
 They are not bad, but practical, and above all, useful.
But the more we think about it,
 we realize they define our whole way of life.
If Yeshua acts this way:
 he took,
 he gave thanks,
 he broke,
 he gave away,
we disciples act this way:
 we feared,
 we complained,
 we fled,
 we hid.

Our usual mode of operation? Yes?
Can we see where it leads us in terms of life?
Whenever we read the gospels, let's place ourselves as
  the disciples.
 They are open to the teaching, but woefully stuck in
  the world.

In the second account, Yeshua approaches the disciples
  with the question.

Again they respond as before:
    they fear there is not enough.
They cling to this attitude in spite of the fact:
    they have already beheld
    the first feeding of the multitude.
Yeshua wants to teach something here.
He is not performing a miracle to show his glory;
    he wishes to instruct us how to respond to any situation
    where we naturally feel lacking or inadequate.
John nails it in his account by confiding that
the question was posed by Yeshua *to test him.*
How would we respond to this test?
We have already witnessed one such multiplication.
    Have we learned the lesson?
What lesson does Yeshua desire to impart to us here?

Chapter 15

THE IMPORTANCE OF GRATITUDE

What if we see Yeshua's actions not as some miracle
    but as a way to usher Love's Dominion into our world?
What if, instead of our usual attitude that there is not
        enough,
    we could simply receive what we have and accept it.
    What if we could bless it, simply give thanks for it?
We are back to grace at meals:
    what if that perfunctory act became a meaningful
        spiritual work?
How might our life be transformed?

Having given thanks for the gift, we can break it up and
        give it away.
Such actions would strike at the core of our fears of
        scarcity.
But what if?
    Might we not find as in the gospel
    that there is more than enough to go around?

When the disciples collect the leftovers, they filled twelve
    baskets—
  a number of fullness—
    twelve tribes of Israel,
    twelve months in the year,
    twelve signs of the Zodiac.

In each story, Yeshua gives the disciples a part to play.
They distribute the bread and fish so they can witness the
    multiplication.
He involves them in the action. It is not a miracle reserved
    to him.
It is an action which he wants his disciples,
    and us their descendants, to share.

Make this series of actions part of everyday practice.
We need not change anything but our attitude.
Instead of falling back into the old pattern
    of scarcity, and playing out that script,
    try this new script:
Receive what we have been given. Truly give thanks for it.
Then break it up and share it with others.
Begin with small things to gain confidence.

What do we not have enough of?
    Time?
    Patience?

Intelligence?
Money?
Find something to work on,
    something modest.
Then test it out.

Acknowledge what we have been given.
    We often do not even know how much we actually
        have,
    so fearful are we.
Then come to the realization that this is a gift given by God.
    Nothing do we possess by nature,
    including our next breath.
Now practice giving thanks for it.
    Keep the action pure.
    Give thanks. That's all.
    No room here for kvetching.
Or asking for more.
    No whining that we don't have enough.
Gratitude must be sincere and from our heart.
    Everything is a gift. As we begin to realize this our
        gratitude grows.
Once we have given thanks, consider ways
    we can break up this gift to share with others.
What steps could we take, if only we had enough?
    Take that step.
But take it from a stance of gratitude and trust.

Try it out in small matters
and develop the trust to bring it to larger things.

For example,
we may feel we do not have enough time
to add prayer and meditation to our life:
a very common experience in beginning a spiritual
discipline.
Now take ten minutes a day to devote to meditation.
Don't worry about how to fit it in. Just do it.
By adding the extra meditation time we
are in a sense breaking up our time and giving it away.
As we become used to the meditation,
we can increase the time.
Then notice what happens to the sense of time
as we continue this practice of thanksgiving.
People report that their sense of time seems to
expand.
They are able to find time for other things.
They do not waste time as they had before.
The only way to know is to try it.

As we gain experience in the practice of meditation,
carry this practice of thanksgiving into other areas of
life.

Add grace before meals, but make it a conscious practice.
Take time throughout the day to give thanks for whatever
      is gift.
See how life begins to expand, multiply, and fill up!
What is important is that thanksgiving eventually
      becomes
   our accustomed script.
Gradually it replaces the "I don't have enough" complaint.

What if we take this story and apply it to today's world?
   How might things change?
Most people go to bed hungry each night.
We throw away food because it is more than we can
      consume.
   Is there no way out of this stupidity?
We can start with ourselves. How can we begin to use
      what we need
   instead of what we think we need or what we want?
Start eating less. Eat more sensibly—foods that do not
      exhaust the earth.
Take the money saved and give it to the hungry.
As one in the service of Love's Dominion,
we will find friends who share this new viewpoint.
We will support one another in our attempts to simplify life,
and together we can witness to others of Love's Dominion.
When every morsel of food is truly seen as God's gift
   how can it happen that so many of Love's children
      starve?

What can we do?
What can we not do?

A journalist once asked Dr. Martin Luther King, Jr.,
"How do you manage to accomplish all that you do
    during the course of a day?"
"I give my first hour to God,"
he said, "and God gives me the rest."

Chapter 16

ABOVE ALL, FORGIVE

Forgive us our sins, as we forgive those who sin against us.

This is the only phrase in the prayer
to which Yeshua adds commentary.
Forgiveness only works when passed on.

*And whenever you pray, forgive, if you have anything against any
one;*
so that your Papa also may forgive you.

For if you forgive people their sins,
your heavenly Papa also will forgive you;
but if you do not forgive people their sins,
neither will your Papa forgive you.

Unless the pardon we receive
in turn flows outward to friend, neighbor, even enemy,
Yeshua says,
there can be no forgiveness at all.

Grudges,
wrongs,
misgivings,
retributions,
vengeance,
    cement the world, and foster our climate of misery.
Love's Dominion is without such "realities."
It is thoroughly grounded in forgiveness;
    between God and humanity,
    one human and another,
    one group and another.
No place here for boundaries. Forgiveness has no
       stopping-place.
It grounds the very life we share in common:
    makes such an existence possible.

We have no problem receiving God's forgiveness.
Most are quite willing and eager for that.
    No strings attached.
    All debts forgiven.
    Chance at a new start.
Who in their right mind would refuse such an offer?

But what if the catch is we in turn must forgive all debts,
    all slights against us?
We extend a new beginning to those who have hurt us.
Feel the resistance rising? Hold on; it gets worse!

A decent man asked Yeshua to dinner;
  Yeshua went into his house and took his place at table.
Then a woman of the city, a sinner, learned he was there,
  and brought an alabaster flask of ointment,
  and standing behind him at his feet,
  weeping, she began to wet his feet with her tears,
  wiped them with her hair, kissed his feet, anointed them.

Imagine we are this good man.
We enjoy a certain prestige in town.
Yeshua is a celebrated teacher, and we have nabbed the
        honor
of hosting him in our house for dinner and talk.
Then this woman appears uninvited
    and upstages everyone with tears and dramatics.
We are bound to have feelings:
    embarrassed for the teacher,
    angry with the woman,
    furious at the servants who gave her entrance.
We may also be irritated with Yeshua for allowing the
        scene to continue
rather than rebuking this interloper.

The host said to himself,
"If this man were a prophet, he would have known who
    and what sort of woman this is who is touching him,
    for she is a sinner."

And Yeshua answering said to him, "Simon, I have something to
say to you."
And he answered, "What is it, Teacher?"

Always beware when Yeshua has something to say;
we are being challenged, put on the spot.
Sure enough:

"A certain creditor had two debtors;
one owed five hundred dollars, and the other fifty.
When they could not pay, he forgave them both.
Now which of them will love him more?"

When Yeshua sets us up in a parable
don't try to second guess him.
We probably know the right answer
thanks to two millennia of Christianity.
But our psyche, which Yeshua hopes to expose for us,
knows the worldly answer.
Only then will we be able to see beyond to the Rule of Love.

Simon answered, "The one, I suppose, to whom he forgave
more."
And he said to him, "You have judged rightly."
Then turning toward the woman he said to Simon,
"Do you see this woman?
I entered your house, you gave me no water for my feet,

> *but she wet my feet with her tears and wiped them with*
> *her hair.*
> *You gave me no kiss,*
> *but from the time I came in, she has not ceased to kiss my*
> *feet.*
> *You did not anoint my head with oil,*
> *but she has anointed my feet with ointment.*
> *Therefore I tell you, her sins, though many, are forgiven,*
> *for she loved much;*
> *but the person forgiven little, loves little."*

Is Yeshua right?

Will a person whose sins are many love much?

Will a person with little to forgive figure forgiveness
no big deal?

If we do not fathom the fantastic mystery of forgiveness
because we feel we aren't great sinners,
perhaps we need extra assistance.

The woman's sins are public: her neighbors condemned
her.

Perhaps Simon's sins are just as great, but hidden,
or even approved by society.

If he cannot begin to recognize the depths of his sinfulness,
how can he be helped and forgiven?

> *Yeshua said to her, "Your sins are forgiven."*
> *Then those at table with him began to whisper,*

"Who is this, who even forgives sins?"
Yeshua told the woman, "Your trust has made you whole; go in
peace."

Just what would it mean for this woman's sins to be
forgiven?
Yeshua has forgiven her—a role reserved to God alone.
But what would happen if her sins were truly forgiven?
She would be welcomed back into her community.
Her past would be forgotten; she would be given a fresh
start.
Problem is, societies do not operate this way.
They aren't in the forgiveness business.
We need a new community, an association founded on
pardon.
Within this new society, the woman would find support
and help in beginning again.
The community would assure its members of their own
forgiveness,
and inspire them to allow forgiveness to flow outward to
others.
But this would involve a serious change.
How will those find forgiveness
whose sin is not against us but against society?
Can we forgive the criminal?
Even if we could, what would that forgiveness matter
if the transgressor is dumped back
into the same world which led to crime?

For Love's Domain to come among us,
it must come on more
    than simply an individual level.
That's no reason to postpone
    adopting radical forgiveness in our own life.
This teaching alerts us to seek out
a community of forgiveness
where others will show us we are indeed known and
        forgiven,
where we will be strengthened, where we can practice
        forgiveness,
and where together we can rehabilitate
those needing public forgiveness.

Chapter 17

WHO IS MY
NEIGHBOR?

Just how far does this obligation to forgive extend?
Obviously we should forgive members of our own family.
And it would be good to extend the circle of forgiveness out
    to include our neighbors as well.
But where does it stop?
How far out must I reach to include people as my neighbor
    for whom I bear responsibility?

But the young man, desiring to justify himself,
said to Yeshua, "And who is my neighbor?"

In a different context, Peter also wanted to test the limits.

Then Peter came and said to him,
    "Lord, if another member of the community sins against me,
    how often should I forgive? As many as seven times?"
Yeshua said to him,
    "Not seven times, but, I tell you, seventy-seven times."

These are legitimate questions; genuine human concerns:
Just what is this way going to cost me?
How much must I extend myself?

We will consider Yeshua's answer to Peter on the extent of
         forgiveness later.
Here let us focus on the question, "Who is my neighbor?"
To this question, Yeshua answers:

> *"A man was going down from Jerusalem to Jericho,*
> *and he fell among robbers,*
> > *who stripped him and beat him,*
> > *and departed, leaving him half dead.*
>
> *Now by chance a priest was going down that road;*
> > *and when he saw him he passed by on the other side.*
>
> *So likewise a Levite, when he came to the place and saw him,*
> > *passed by on the other side.*
>
> *But a Samaritan, as he journeyed, came to where he was;*
> > *and when he saw him, he had compassion,*
> > *and went to him and bound up his wounds,*
> > *pouring on oil and wine;*
> > *then he set him on his own beast and brought him to an*
> > > *inn,*
> > *and took care of him.*
>
> *And the next day he took out a generous sum of money*
> *and gave them to the innkeeper, saying,*
> > *'Take care of him;*
> > *and whatever more you spend, I will repay you when I*
> > > *come back.'*

Which of these three, do you think,
proved neighbor to the man who fell among the robbers?"
He said, "The one who showed mercy on him."
Yeshua said, "Go and do likewise."

Notice how Yeshua turns the question around.

The young man, who wants to be told he is doing well,
asks a question wondering how far he has to stretch
himself:
"Who qualifies as my neighbor and therefore
deserves my help?"

Yeshua turns the understanding of neighbor around:

The neighbor is the one who reaches out with help and
compassion.

And Yeshua asks the more important question:

Are we acting as a neighbor?

In the parable, only the least likely person acts neighborly.

The priest and Levites were respected members of the
community:
models of holy living.

Yet they do not act neighborly to the fallen man.

Only the Samaritan, the heretic, the outcast, is a neighbor.

Let's consider to whom he reaches out in help.

The man fallen among thieves is most likely an Israelite.

He is separated from the Samaritan
by a long history of dissention and distrust.

Besides, he is an idiot:

no one in their right mind would walk that road
from Jerusalem to Jericho alone.
It's a wild, deserted region;
notorious for harboring thieves and cutthroats.
This jerk asks for it! He gets just what he deserves.

Now here come the other three. They too are in great
danger.
Would we really trust that the man in the dust is hurt?
Maybe he is faking it to trick and rob us.
Maybe his cohorts, thieves, are hiding nearby,
waiting for us to come to his aid, so they can jump us
too.
All these factors seem to cancel the obligation to be a
neighbor.

But the Samaritan takes the risk; he goes all the way.
Notice how Yeshua piles up phrase after phrase,
describing the Samaritan's deeds toward
the man fallen among thieves.
Here's what it means to be a neighbor.
It has nothing to do with whether the neighbor is worthy
of our aid.
It has nothing to do with what the neighbor might think of us.
It has only to do with helping whomever we come upon in
need.

Only so do we represent, mirror forth, show others
    the presence and glory of Love's Domain.

Consider another way of reading this fascinating story.
Who might that man fallen among thieves be?
    Some see him as Yeshua himself.
The fallen man, who acted stupidly, who suffered a brutal
      fate,
    is actually the one who brings a vision of a new way
      of living.
Lying there helpless, he provides us the opportunity
    to move out of our accustomed course of action.
In helping the man, the Samaritan
    discovers the wonders of Love's Dominion.
The opportunity was extended to priest and Levite as well,
    but they could not sense the opportunity,
    only the obligation;
they did the sensible human thing;
    they passed by on the other side.

The Way of Yeshua is not obvious.
It is hidden within the everyday;
    the tedious tasks of daily life.
Love offers us constant opportunities
    to encounter this Domain.
But most seem occasions better avoided.
We elect to pass by on the other side. What might we miss
      in doing so?

I was hungry
    and you gave me food,
I was thirsty
    and you gave me drink,
I was a stranger
    and you welcomed me,
I was naked
    and you clothed me,
I was sick
    and you visited me,
I was in prison
    and you came to me.

"Lord, when did we see you hungry
    and feed you,
or thirsty
    and give you drink?
When did we see you a stranger
    and welcome you,
or naked
    and clothe you?
When did we see you sick or in prison
    and visit you?"

In truth I tell you
    as you did it to one of the least
    of these my brothers and sisters,
    you did it to me.

Many opportunities exist to encounter Love's Dominion.
God wears the face of anyone in trouble.
People marveled how Mother Teresa
    could care for those shunned by all.
How could she nurse people doomed to die?
How could she abide to be around people in such terrible
      suffering?
"But when I see these people," she said, "I do not see them.
    I see Yeshua, my beloved. How could I not care for
      him."
It is truly wonderful and strange how Love's Dominion
      comes to us,
    and invites us to enter through the simple act
    of becoming neighbor to all.

Chapter 18

THE PROBLEM IS US

At first glance, forgiveness seems wonderful,
    especially as we look forward to a new start for
        ourselves.
But it is also a great stumbling block.
It is one thing to be forgiven;
    another to forgive as we have been forgiven.
There's the rub.
But Yeshua adamantly connects the two:
Being forgiven is contingent upon forgiving in turn.

Love's Dominion is like
a master who wanted to settle accounts with his servants.
One who owed ten thousand dollars was brought forward.
He could not pay, so the king ordered him sold
    along with his wife and family and all he had,
    to make payment.
The servant fell on his knees, and begged,
    "Lord, have patience with me,
    and I will pay you everything."
Out of compassion the lord released him and forgave the debt.

So far, so good.

We should be able to easily slip into the role of the servant.

We can feel real gratitude and appreciation for such a
master.

From what would we like relief?

What weighs upon us? From what past burdens do we
seek release?

But that same servant went out,
and met a fellow servant who owed him a hundred dollars;
seizing him by the throat he said, "Pay what you owe me."
So his fellow servant fell down and begged him,
"Have patience with me, and I will pay you."

Yeshua sets it up beautifully.

The first scene is played out again;
only the characters have changed.

We might, even as we inhabit the first servant's skin,
sense a certain *deja vu* here.

But feel the weight of this servant's need.

Obviously he is not rich or he would have been able to
repay his debt.

He needs that money. Besides there may be other worries.

Is this friend trying to get away with something?

Is he trying to default?

Yeshua offers a glimpse of ourselves
    and what prevents entering Love's Dominion.
Let's say that, like the servant in the story,
    we refuse to cancel our friend's debt.
What happens?

> *He refused and went and put him in prison*
>   *till he should pay the debt.*
> *When his fellow servants saw what had taken place,*
>   *they were greatly distressed.*
> *They reported to their lord all that had taken place.*
> *Then his lord summoned him and said, "You wicked servant!*
>   *I forgave you all that debt because you begged me;*
>   *and should not you have had mercy on your fellow servant,*
>   *as I had mercy on you?"*
> *And in anger his lord delivered him to the jailers,*
>   *till he should pay all his debt.*
> *So shall my heavenly Father do to every one of you,*
>   *if you do not forgive your brother or sister from your heart.*

There's a line to make skin crawl.
We'll meet a number of these disturbing parables.
But keep in mind that they are not meant to condemn.
They are a medicine to help us surrender the world for
    Love's Domain.

Take a good look at this servant.
Observe the aspects of ourselves

that resonate with the servant.
Is this really who we are?
Yes, in the midst of battle
    we may find ourselves acting this way,
    but is this the very core of our being?

One difficulty in grasping this story:
    we have little understanding what it means to be a
        servant.
We are uncomfortable with the idea of servants.
    We believe all people are equal.
But in Yeshua's day servants had not yet been
        democratized:
    A servant is but a stand-in for the master.
    He or she is not expected
    or supposed to do anything original.
Represent the master in all things: That's the job!

Modern psychology would call the servant the "ego":
    that aspect of ourselves that identifies itself as who
        we are.
The ego thinks it is the real center of the universe.
    It believes itself invincible.
But it is not, and when it is allowed to run riot, chaos
        ensues.
The Way of Yeshua is a training of the ego in the service
        of the spirit.
Ego must come to see itself as servant, not master.

Consider Yeshua's parable not as a commentary on
    slavery,
but as a description of how we operate.
The Holy Spirit, that divine spark within each creature,
    is of God and acts as God.
What is God like?
    Forgiving. All forgiving.

Spiritual practice makes the servant
    a more accurate representative of the master.
    The servant is tamed, trained.

So in Yeshua's story, the master is forgiving.
If the servant is to be a true servant, an image of the master,
    he or she too must be forgiving.
If the servant is unforgiving, what is to be done?
He is thrown into prison until the last penny is repaid.
This is a figure for the spiritual work we are called to do.
    Don't make it concrete as a place like Hell.
    It is truly hell, but as a state of unforgiveness
    in which we choose to live and which can create only
        misery.

Our own ego does not want to forgive.
    But this is not who we truly are.
    Our spirit is indeed the Holy Spirit, to use the
        Christian term.

So our practice as followers of Yeshua
    consists in becoming aware of what we are doing.
When we realize we are in a situation demanding
       forgiveness,
    can we remember to represent our true self
    rather than the little ego who wants to be in charge?
As we practice letting go of being first
    we will begin to notice a transformation in our life—
    we will move more deeply into Love's Domain.

Chapter 19

EMBRACE THE PRODIGAL

Whe we try to practice forgiveness,
    sooner or later we encounter resentment.
It usually manifests in someone close to us,
    a family member.
We know them too well.
    We believe they are getting away with something.
We freeze forgiveness toward them. Our rancor festers.
Only people close enough and present enough
    have the power to provoke resentments.

Yeshua's most famous parable makes the point clear.
It's about a family—a father and two sons.

Once a man had two sons.
The younger said to his father,
    "Give me my share of property now so that I may enjoy
        myself."
So he divided his living between them.

Soon after, the younger son gathered all he had
and went into a far country.
There he squandered his inheritance recklessly.
When he had gone through everything,
a great famine arose, and he began to feel the pinch.
So he went and got a job, in the fields where he fed the pigs.
He would gladly have fed on the pods for the swine;
but no one gave him anything.

He came to himself and said,
"How many of my father's hired hands have bread
enough to spare,
and I am dying here from hunger!
I will arise and go to my father, and say to him,
'Father, I have sinned against both heaven and you;
I am no longer worthy to be called your son;
treat me as one of your hired hands.'"

So he arose and came to his father.
But while he was still far off,
his father saw him and had compassion,
and ran, embraced him, and kissed him.
The son said,
"Father, I have sinned against both heaven and you;
I am no longer worthy to be called your son."
But the father told his servants,
"Quickly bring the best robe,

put it on him;
put a ring on his hand,
shoes on his feet;
bring the fatted calf and kill it,
let us eat and make merry;
for my son who was dead, is alive again;
he was lost, and is found."
And the festivities began.

So far so good.
We can envision ourselves as this younger child.
We feel guilty or ashamed of things in our past.
Wouldn't it be wonderful if we could dare admit our guilt
     to be greeted with such an outpouring of joy and love?

Let's put it into our own family context.
Would our father have acted this way?
Is there something just a little "unreal" about it?
This is not the world, but Love's Domain.
     Too good to be true.
Think so?
     Hold on! Reality is about to enter with a vengeance.

Now the elder son was in the field;
     as he drew near the house, he heard music and dancing.
He called a servant and asked the meaning.
     "Your brother has come,

and your father has killed the fatted calf,
because he has received him safe and sound."
But the boy was angry and refused to go in.
His father came out and pleaded with him,
but he answered,

"I've served you all my life, and I never disobeyed you;
yet you never gave me a goat,
so I could party with my friends.
But this son of yours comes home;
he's devoured your living with whores,
and you kill the fatted calf for him!"
"Son, you are always with me, and all I have is yours.
It was fitting to party and celebrate,
for this your brother was dead, and is alive;
he was lost, and is found."

This brother resembles us
more than we might care to admit.
But we gain nothing by shrinking from the images.
Only by facing them can we find healing.

Let's look into our own life.
Find someone against whom we hold a resentment.
If we can find no one, we are kidding ourselves.
Look at the people close to us—
mother, father,
brother, sister,
in-laws, co-workers, friends.

We know someone who has wronged us.
If we come up empty in the present consider the past,
    especially our childhood,
        before we learned to hide resentments.

Go into the feeling. Let the sensations expand.
What is good about this emotion?
What does it profit us to hold on to it?
    There must be some payoff or we wouldn't cling to it.
What is bad about it? What might it cost to let it go?

Go back to the parable's ending.
But there is no ending!
Yeshua leaves us hanging. "Work it out for yourselves!"
Consider the possibilities! What could we do?
We could turn our back on the whole charade.
    Stomp off to the barn and sulk.
    Or even pack and leave.
In either case, we preserve our integrity and sense of justice.
If Junior absconds with the rest of the money, we can gloat.

But what do we lose?
For one thing, we miss out on the party.
We will never taste that fatted calf.

The only opportunity to enjoy the festivities truly
    seems to be to drop our own sense of outrage

and, like our father, forgive the kid.
Let bygones be bygones. Bring on the meat.
This may appear the hardest choice of all
    but is it not truly the best,
      the only one that offers happiness?

Now enter the story more deeply, not in terms of family
    but as an image of the human psyche.
The younger brother plays the ego:
    like the servant in the last parable
    who runs headlong into ruin.
And the elder brother?
    Mr. Prim-and-Proper, careful and cautious,
    the super-ego:
    the voice that spells out for us right and wrong.
He never acts up or out.
In many of us, this aspect rules.
Few of us really qualify as the younger son.
For one thing, younger sons don't study spirituality.
    They're off having fun.
The older brother is more like most of us;
    and he wants to disinherit that disreputable juvenile in
      ourselves and others.

But there is another component to the story
    and to our own psyche:
The Father—
    the wisdom figure who holds the whole together.

Pass over into his viewpoint now.
Here are our two sons—
>one was lost and is found,
>the other now will not set foot in the house
>to greet and welcome his brother.
Feel the pain of both sons.
And feel our own pain:
>as a father we want to embrace them both in our love.
Can we sense in ourselves the need to reconcile these two wayward boys?
Can we move up into the father's viewpoint
>and see how trapped in self these kids are?
Now shift back to our own life carrying the father's experience.
Might this figure help us drop our resentment
>and begin to enjoy the party?
The celebration is here whether we are ready or not.
>Price of admission? Lighten up!

Chapter 20

LOVE EVEN ENEMIES

The elder brother thinks: My brother is the enemy.

He had to come to realize this is not the enemy
but my brother.

Our brother we thought dead has come back.
Come, let's celebrate!

So in our own families,
    the place where people are close
    and intimate enough to hurt us,
We must remember these are not enemies,
    but brothers and sisters.
Drop the fortifications, and embrace as family.

But Yeshua goes much further.
He tells us to look at our real enemies
    and see them too as brothers and sisters.

We are moving beyond good and evil, right and wrong.
Judgment has no place in Love's Dominion.
The other person is a creature of God,
 a beloved creation and so my brother or sister.
No one here is evil.
 Difference, yes,
 Diversity, of course.
 Enemies, no.

"People say, 'You shall love your neighbor and hate your enemy.'
But I say, Love your enemies; pray for those who persecute you,
 so that you may be children of Papa;
 who makes the sun rise on the evil and on the good,
 and sends rain on the just and on the unjust.
If you love those who love you, what do you gain?
Do not even thieves do the same?
If you greet only your friends,
 what more are you doing than others?
You, therefore, must be whole and all-encompassing,
 as your heavenly Papa is whole and all-encompassing."

How difficult to see this from our present perspective!
This teaching seems idealistic, impossible to realize—
 even in a community where everyone tries to follow
  the same vision
 let alone one where we don't share such a viewpoint.
To act this way asks to be manipulated, taken advantage of.

God makes the sun rise on both the just and the unjust
and the rain fall on both equally.

When I am limited to myself,
I am not able to allow you entrance.
You are the other; your needs threaten my own.
But if I can imagine both of us as children of Love
    and begin to perceive from Love's perspective,
    I can move toward a more inclusive vision.
We can begin to work to expand our own limited egoistic
        horizons.
How does what I do affect others?
How might I take a more embracing look
    at the situation between me and another?
What might be good for both of us rather than myself alone?
We are moving from me first to we first.
    And that "we" is without limits.

Just to begin the practice of expanding our own horizons
    is part of this work.
That does not automatically mean
    that we will be able to put it into practice here and now.

After all, we are living in the world
    although we wish to live by a higher vision.
If someone is out to rip us off,
    acting like a doormat
    will help no one in the long run.
We must live in the world but not of it.

And we will want to apply these teachings
    to a different degree in different situations.
In the family, hopefully,
      we will be able to share the vision of Love's Domain
      so that we may practice loving others as ourselves
        most of the time.
However we don't entrust the auto mechanic
    with the same amount of faith we do our spouse.
See him as a neighbor, but examine his bills with a
    discerning eye.

There may come times
    when we dare use this teaching to subvert the world.
The world is founded on judgments:
    If one is a friend,
    there must be another who is the enemy.
What happens when we begin to drop these judgments
    from our thoughts and actions?
This so-called enlightened age hangs onto a great deal of
      prejudice—
    against the opposite sex, people of other colors,
    other religions, other languages and customs,
    other sexual orientations.
What kind of spiritual work might help us
    see and move beyond our remaining prejudices?
How might we get to know some of these people
    so that we may come to see them as brothers and sisters
    sharing our unity as Love's children?

Do we view the world as "us" vs. "them,"
   whoever "they" might be?
Do these feelings affect what we say or when we speak out?
What do we teach our children about our common unity
      in Love?
When they pick up stereotypes and derogatory remarks
      from their peers
   how do we teach them to recognize the hurt there
   and move toward embracing the other?
What do we say when someone else acts with bias?
Do we keep our peace
   or do we show discomfort with prejudice?
Do we support people perceived as other
   socially or politically?

I remember an embarrassing incident that brought to
      mind that
   the "enemy" is my brother.
I was driving home on the freeway
   and as I approached my exit
   a car dawdled in front of me.
Too late to pass him; I was stuck following:
   as usual I was in a hurry.
That driver inspired in me a whole slew of invectives.
Spewing epithets I pulled up alongside at the stoplight by
      the exit.
I looked over only to discover a dear friend.
Instantly the situation changed
   although I had not done anything public to express
      my rage,

151

I felt ashamed and guilty.
How could I think these things about him?
    I had seen him as an obstacle, not a brother.
It is the same with the other no matter the situation,
    from the person ahead of us in line, to our age-old
        enemy.
Whoever it is, they have the same concerns, fears,
    gifts, and shortcomings we all do.
Just another human being trying to do their best,
    a fellow sufferer of life,
    a brother or sister at heart,
    at least in the heart of God.

Chapter 21

EXTEND YOURSELF FURTHER

During supper . . .
Yeshua . . .

rose from the table,
laid aside his garments,
fastened a towel around his waist.
Then he poured water into a basin
and began to wash the disciples' feet
and to wipe them with the towel.
When he had washed their feet,
taken his garments, and resumed his place,
he said, "Do you know what I have done to you?
You call me Teacher and Lord; and you are right; I am.
If I then, your Lord and Teacher, have washed your feet,
you also should wash each other's feet.
I have given you an example, which you also should do
as I have done to you.
Indeed, I say, a servant is not greater than the master;
nor is the one who is sent greater than the one who sends.
If you know these things, blessed are you if you do them."

How radical!
He, the teacher, the leader, becomes a mere servant.
Washing his disciples' feet, an ordinary action before dining,
   is totally inappropriate to the master.

Yet Yeshua washes his disciples' feet.
And he commands us to continue this custom in our
      community.
It takes a great deal of humility to perform this action—
   one would need to be "poor in spirit" indeed
   not to balk at such a menial, lowly task.

A dispute also arose among them:
    who was to be regarded as the greatest.
Yeshua said, "Pagan leaders exercise lordship over them;
those in authority are called benefactors.
But it shall not be so with you;
    whoever would be great among you must be your servant,
    whoever would be first among you must serve everyone.
For who is greater, one who sits at table, or one who serves?
Is it not the one who sits at table? But I am among you as one
    who serves.
You must do to one another as I have done to you.

Sense how this grates against who we are,
   our own dignity and self-respect.
Who would want to live like this?

We do not trust ourselves to servant leadership.
Yeshua's model has not been tried and found deficient.
It has been found repulsive, at best ridiculous,
    and seldom, if ever,
    put into practice outside church rituals.

You are not to be called "teacher," for you have one teacher,
    and you are all brothers and sisters.
And call no one your father on earth,
    for you have one Papa, who is in heaven.
Whoever is greatest among you shall be your servant;
whoever exalts themselves will be humbled,
    and whoever humbles themselves will be exalted.

Can we expect any organization to last
    given such a shocking abdication of authority?
We don't know; it has never been tried.
What has been tried, even in churches, is the earthly model.
And things end up worse than the secular model
    because it tampers with people's spirits—
the churches try to cage what is ultimately free.
The spirit blows where it wills.

Consider the inconceivable!
How might this servant leadership work
    in the family,
    at work,
    in the helping professions,

in religious organizations?
What problems would it cause if it were implemented?

And, if we don't believe it would cause problems, we
        don't have a clue
    what servant leadership is.
What would be success? What would be failure?
What could be done concerning retaliation and persecution?
How might we help servant leadership prevail in the face
        of the world?

People say,
    "An eye for an eye and a tooth for a tooth."
But I say,
    Do not resist one who is evil.
    But if any one strikes you on the right cheek,
    turn the other also;
    and if any one would sue you and take your coat,
    surrender your cloak as well;
    and if any one forces you to go one mile,
    go with him two miles.
Give to those who beg from you,
    and do not refuse those who would borrow from you.

Yeshua seems to ask us not only to lie down
    and suffer the world to walk over us
    but to scrape the mud off its boots as well.

We misunderstand, though, because we do not know
    the actual social situation in which Yeshua taught.
As a political colony of Rome, Palestinians were under laws
    as to what the Roman occupation could demand of
      them.
A Roman soldier could force a colonial to accompany
    him for a mile
    and carry his supplies.
Should the supplies be transported further
    the soldier would have exceeded the legal limit
    and be liable to punishment.
At least one purpose of such a teaching, then,
    might be to foster seeming compliance
    while at the same time creating trouble for the
      occupation.
That is the spirit of these teachings.

Yeshua has hit on the power of noncompliance
    which differs from resistance.
When we resist we oppose one force with another.
In noncompliance, we offer no resistance
    and can actually turn the force against itself.
Asian martial arts build upon just this truth.
The small unarmed monk is able to defeat the huge
    armed warrior.
The greater the warrior's strength,
    the more force he encounters turned upon himself.

Far from merely a truth of physical power in the martial arts,
    it is true of power universally.
It lies behind Love's refusal to go against evil.
This is the truth at the heart of all revolutions as well.
When the powerless, who have the truth, achieve power
they lose that very truth
    as those oppressed become oppressors.

This astounding teaching applies in almost every area.
After all, its power inspired two twentieth-century
        revolutions.
Gandhi used it to remove the British from control of India,
and Martin Luther King, Jr., used it to fuel the early civil
        rights movement.
Both revolutions accomplished far more through
        nonviolence
    than normal force could achieve.

The principle works in small situations as well.
Consider how the idea that another person is our enemy
    transforms not only our own perception of that person,
    but the entire situation in which we are involved.
If I see you as the enemy who is out to get me
    and whom I must subdue in order to get my own way,
    there is not much hope of a creative outcome.
The most powerful person wins;
    whether that side embraces truth is irrelevant.

Is there another way we can practice
    approaching such situations?
Can I see myself for just who I am?
    One fallible, questioning person.
And can I begin to see you as just such another?
Can I, until I am conclusively shown to be wrong,
    presume good will on your part
    and offer good will on my own?
If we come together, we may realize we have a common
       problem
    and we each have ways of viewing that problem and
       its solutions,
but we can also admit that the problem is ours together
    and the task at solving it is also ours together.
Solving the problem need not involve one person winning;
    a solution agreeable to both is possible
    which may move the whole issue to a deeper level.

Chapter 22

WORK FOR JUSTICE

"**I**f you want peace, work for justice,"
said Pope Paul VI.
But just what is justice in Love's Dominion?
When we encounter Love's Justice,
    we often feel angry, ripped off.
Indeed, Love's justice is a stumbling block.

Love's Dominion is like a landowner
    who went out early in the morning
        to hire laborers for his vineyard.
After agreeing with the laborers for the usual daily wage,
    he sent them into his vineyard.
When he went out about nine o'clock,
    he saw others standing idle in the marketplace;
and he said to them,
    "You also go into the vineyard,
        and I will pay you whatever is right."
So they went.
When he went out again about noon and about three o'clock,
    he did the same.

161

And about five o'clock he went out
    and found others standing around;
and he said to them, "Why are you standing here idle all day?"
They said to him, "Because no one has hired us."
He said to them, "You also go into the vineyard."
When evening came, the owner of the vineyard
said to his manager, "Call the laborers and give them their pay,
    beginning with the last and then going to the first."
When those hired about five o'clock came,
    each received the usual daily wage.
Now when the first came,
    they thought they would receive more;
    but each of them also received the usual daily wage.
And when they received it,
    they grumbled against the landowner,
saying, "These last worked only one hour,
    and you have made them equal to us
    who have borne the burden of the day
    and the scorching heat."
But he replied to one of them, "Friend, I am doing you no wrong;
    did you not agree with me for the usual daily wage?
    Take what belongs to you and go;
    I choose to give to this last the same as I give to you.
    Am I not allowed to do
    what I choose with what belongs to me?
    Or are you envious because I am generous?"
So the last will be first, and the first will be last.

How does that grab us?
If we envision ourselves as last hired, it is too good to be
      true.
We have family to feed, and one hour's wage won't do it.
But what if we are the ones who have worked through the
      scorching heat?
How can we help but be galled,
    that these "Johnny-come-latelys" are getting the
      same as we are?
Yeshua knows human nature.

Our sense of justice is intimately tied up to our sense of self.
If we find ourselves in the position of the five o'clock
      laborers
    or the prodigal son,
we hope mercy will bail us out.
But if we believe we did something worthwhile,
    we are quick to look for acknowledgment and reward,
    like those hired first, or the elder son.
Our first cry will be "Where's the justice in this?"
Well, where's the mercy in our justice?

The landlord gives people what they need,
    not what they deserve.
The father of the prodigal son did the same.
That provides a rich hint of Love's justice.
And it is hard to swallow.

But as in the Prodigal Son, what are we going to do?
Do we throw down our hard-earned money in disgust,
    to preserve our sense of human dignity?
In that case, our family goes hungry!

We have no say if the landlord chooses to be generous.
And Love is unbelievably generous.
If we would abide in Love's Dominion,
our sense of justice
must exceed the bounds of ego and self.
Those hired at five o'clock may well be lazy.
They just didn't think anyone would hire them.
How do we address the underlying issues
    which create inequity and injustice in our society?
If we enroll in the service of Love's Dominion,
    such affairs become our concern.

Yeshua is in harmony with his tradition here.
That tradition not only tells people to be kind
    and to treat others as they would be treated.
It goes further to highlight especially the plight of
    the widow, the orphan, the stranger.
They too must be cared for.
These are the traditionally forgotten, marginal people of
        the time.
Yeshua acted this out by befriending
    tax collectors who extorted from their neighbors
        to collaborate with the Romans,

prostitutes, and lepers.
He gathers an unsavory bunch around him,
    showing that Love knows no boundaries to its care
        and concern.
Justice is for all and based on need,
    rather than some imagined earned worth.

Chapter 23

SURRENDER
JUDGMENT

Does the mercy we see in the parable of the laborers
mean injustice is allowed to prevail?
Don't we have a mission to see that the world operates
according to the truths of Love?
Is it not our responsibility as people who know Love's will
to ensure that will is carried out?

From such thinking, many great harms arise.
It is not up to us to reconcile
Love's justice with Love's mercy.
Enough for us to be merciful.
So we enter into Love's Domain.
Leave the justice
and its inevitable correlate "judgment" to Love.

Judge not,
and you will not be judged;
condemn not,

and you will not be condemned;
forgive,
> *and you will be forgiven;*
give,
> *and it will be given to you;*
good measure,
> *pressed down,*
> *shaken together,*
> *running over,*
> *will flow into your lap.*
For the measure you give
> *will be the measure you get back.*

Reciprocation runs through this saying.
Act with judgment, without condemnation,
> with forgiveness, and generosity
> and we will experience the same in turn.
How light this makes our task!
What has happened to this teaching?
As soon as we escape the blade of judgment,
> we want to reposition it over our neighbor.

Take Yeshua at his word. He does not stand alone.
> Paul echoes this admonition not to judge.
What would happen if we were to withdraw from the
> judgment game?

What would happen if we admitted we are totally
    incompetent to judge?
That's precisely what Yeshua tells us.

> *Can a blind man lead a blind man? Will they not both fall into*
>   *a pit?*
> *A disciple is not above his teacher,*
>   *but every one when he is fully taught will be like his*
>   *teacher.*
> *Why do you see the speck in your brother's eye,*
>   *but do not notice the log in your own?*
> *Or how can you tell your brother,*
>   *"Brother, let me take out the speck that is in your eye,"*
> *when you yourself do not see the log in your own eye?*
> *You hypocrite, first take the log out of your own eye,*
>   *then you will see clearly to take the speck out of your*
>   *brother's eye.*

If Yeshua relieves me of the job of judging others,
he also assures me they will not be my judges.
I do not have to act a certain way to impress or win them
    over.
I do not have to live up to their standards.
All I have to do is be myself
    because this is truly all I can do.
Being myself is sufficient and all right.
It is not subject to my or anyone else's judgment.

Examine the role judgment plays in the world.
Everything runs on the machinery of discernment.
It begins almost the moment we leave our mother's
     womb.
There is only a short time when the one response we
     evoke is:
     "What a cute, darling baby!"
Even if they continue to mouth it, secretly they make
     judgments about us.
     Isn't she awfully small? Do you think he's really normal?
     Shouldn't she be walking by now? Talking? Potty
     trained?
More than interest lurks behind these questions.
We are being measured against others or the norm.
We are being judged.
No longer simply a bundle of joy,
     now that bundle must be weighed in the balance.

And we are just at the beginning of a long, seemingly infinite
     series of judgments about us, our capabilities, our
     capacities.
     We lean toward the virtue of judgment. In all our
     institutions,
     from grade school
          (which in some areas today requires entrance
          exams)
     to prisons

(which surrender any pretense of education
    in favor of the strictest interpretation of judgment).
How many schools have given up report cards and grades
    as inadequate means to assess a student's progress?
How many prisons have given up any hope of rehabilitation
    for a stringent program of punishment,
    retribution, and incarceration?

Judgment has progressed from a simple process of
    making distinctions
    to the very foundation of the world itself.
Judgment determines who will be on top
    and who on the bottom.
It invents these categories in the first place,
    then goes about remaking the entire world in its image.
It goes far beyond discernment to sort people
    into types and categories
    which then are used to impose limits upon them.
Thank God sometimes people slip
    through our categories' cracks.
Einstein was a poor student in the lower grades, especially
    bad at math.
He would have been judged a poor store clerk, let alone
    an astrophysicist.
Judgments create boundaries necessary to conduct
    a certain kind of thought,
but they become prisons if mistaken for reality.

We are all truly without boundaries. We are not limited.
We are free and spontaneous. Do not let judgment fence
us in.
Helen Keller, deaf, dumb, and blind,
leavened the world with her indomitable spirit.

Am I really claiming God has withdrawn from the
judgment business?
Is that so strange?
Love allows us to overlook every defect.

Chapter 24

THE JOYS OF PERSECUTION

What are we going to do about judgment in our own
    lives?
Can we afford to simply let the world go its merry way?
Most of us can't. We are too tied to it for our well-being.
And the world does not respond gratefully
    to those who point out its lack of reality.
Yeshua is quite aware of this.
Consider his own end,
    which at least for him was no surprise.
We have to consider the consequences of following his
        path.
He doesn't downplay our effect upon the world:

> *Happy are you when people revile you*
> *and persecute you and utter all kinds of evil*
> *against you falsely on my account.*
> *Rejoice and be glad, for your reward is great in Love's Domain,*
> *for in the same way they persecuted the prophets who were*

before you.
You are the salt of the earth;
> *but if salt has lost its taste, how can its saltiness be*
> *restored?*
It is no longer good for anything,
> *but is thrown out and trampled under foot.*
You are the light of the world. A city built on a hill cannot be hid.
No one after lighting a lamp puts it under the bushel basket,
> *but on the lampstand, and it gives light to all in the house.*
In the same way, let your light shine before others,
> *so that they may see your good works and give glory to*
> *Love.*

Until Love's Domain arrives in power, we must ask
> ourselves
> what is our own relationship to the world
> with its machinery of judgment.
No comfortable solution is available.
On the one hand, it is not possible
> to experience Love's Domain in its fullness just yet.
On the other hand, we will not simply surrender to the
> world;
> that would destroy our spirit and betray our mission.
We must learn to live in the world but not be a part of it:
> a delicate maneuver to say the least.
At times we are compelled to play judgment games.
'f we want any worldly position, we must submit to
> its various forms of judgment.

Once in position we must abide by the guidelines to a
    certain extent.
But we do not have to take this judgment business
    seriously.
Does what somebody or some institution says about me
    really reflect who I am?
Am I to be judged by my beauty,
    my ancestors, my religion,
    my skin color, my sexuality,
    my intellect, my social skills,
    my cunning, or any other measure?
Can I separate out this obsession with judgment from
    my spiritual life,
    from my spiritual community?
This will not be easy.
We are so accustomed to judgment,
    it becomes the air we breathe.
But we can begin with little things
    such as our spiritual practice.
Do we judge it and evaluate it?
Yes, it is necessary to do it correctly:
    that's what teachers and comrades are for.
But do we go into a meditation and then become upset
    when it doesn't proceed as we expect or want it to?
Do we get excited when it seems to be progressing
    wonderfully?
Each is a judgment.

All we are asked to do is sit and be with
    what is happening now.
No expectations, no critique.
Better simply to be present to the experience.
Drop all judgments on what it is like,
    whether I am doing it well,
    whether I am making progress.
Judgments are exactly what we are working on.
This is the labor itself.

As we gain experience dropping judgment in our practice,
    we will become more aware of judgment
    in ordinary life.
When we find ourselves judging, we can learn to stop and
      question
    whether it is necessary or beneficial.
If I am judging whether a job is being properly done
    this is beneficial.
I do not want to turn out bad products.
But perhaps I am bringing judgment to something
    I do not need to.

What do I think of the weather?
    Does it matter? Can I change it?
    Just be with it. See what happens.

Don't resist the rain and observe whether the experience
    changes.

Someone asked a Chinese sage what it means to be
    enlightened.
    "To have no opinions," was his response.

As we back off from automatic judgments,
    we can begin to bring this process into areas of life
    where judgment does no good, as in child-rearing.
Children need encouragement, love, and acceptance.
They do not need judgment; the world will do enough of
    that.
Can we create a home environment where they might
    experience
    the joy of simply being themselves free from
    judgments?
This is hard.
How can we give up the harsh word in judgment
    for the long, drawn-out process
    of teaching them to see the consequences of their
    behavior?
No one said the Way of Yeshua was easy.

Surrendering judgment, we finally begin to see truly for
    the first time.

Reasons and projections do not color and distort our
    perception.
We can see the act of killing for simply what it is
    and neither condemn it because it is done unlawfully
    or praise it because it was done in the line of duty.
    Both are murder.
Only then can we begin to perceive correctly,
    without society's lenses or our own prejudices.
And as we grow able to see we may be called to speak out—
    to speak the truth of what we see
    in the hope others might listen.

Such an immense mission may daunt us.
Do I really want to change the world?
Isn't this just about finding a more satisfactory life
    for myself and my loved ones?
Yes, it is, but as we make each step of the journey
    our horizons expand and our understanding deepens.
All we need to do is trust right now that
    just as Love is present for us now to aid and guide us,
    Love will be present in our future whatever crossroads
        we face.
Sufficient to the day is the task at hand.
And the task at hand right now is to begin to sniff out
    the ways judgment colors our lives today.

Forget about tomorrow. We are not ready for that now.
And if we do not turn our attention to the work at hand,
we shall never be ready.

Chapter 25

WATCH THAT ANGER

Yeshua provides a number of teachings
    for working with emotions.
His teaching is of the marketplace,
    not of the convent or monastery:
    a teaching for people
    in the midst of common secular life.
Although we may have to draw aside from that life
    in order to pray and practice,
    everything we practice should lead us back
    to the world and others
    as a more complete human being.
Of course, when we relate to others through our emotions
    we play with fire.
    We have a history with relatives, family, and friends.
    They are important to us. We share their lives.
Aware of the risks, let us proceed slowly and cautiously.
Let's work on the small stuff first
    until we have confidence in the teachings.
Then we can move on to the larger issues.

Anger is a very common emotion;
    some claim it is the most prevalent feeling.
Some of us do not believe that we get angry;
    that in itself should alert us to the problem.
If I am not angry at times, something is wrong with me.
I am not connecting with life.
We may feel that anger is forbidden to the spiritual person.
Good people do not get angry:
This is a pious generalization which a quick glance at the
        gospels sets right:
    Yeshua has anger, and he expresses it.
    He chases the moneychangers out of the temple
    and overturns their tables.
    He rants against the scribes and pharisees.
    He curses a fig tree
    when it was not even the season for figs.
Anger itself is not bad or evil. It is a necessary emotion.
When something upsetting happens, we become angry.
Nothing wrong there.
The question is:
    What do we do with our anger?

Beginning in childhood, we are taught to deal with anger.
Perhaps we were not allowed to show or express it.
We learned to hide it inside so that today
    we cannot tell when we are angry.

Now it seeps out in devious destructive ways from ulcers
      to depression.
Perhaps our parents could not contain our anger.
We learned to fear it. It could devour us.
Perhaps we grew dependent upon our anger.
We learned to control everyone with our own wrath.
All these distortions must be confronted as we mature.
We must overcome our fear of it.
We must learn to recognize it:
     and allow its expression in appropriate
rather than destructive ways.
We may need the help of counseling.

For now we can listen to Yeshua's words
     and see how we might begin to apply them
     in our own relationships.

You have heard it said to those of old,
"You shall not kill;
     and whoever kills shall be liable to judgment."
But I say every one who is angry with his brother
     shall be liable to judgment;
whoever insults his brother shall be liable to the council,
and whoever says, "You fool!" shall be liable to the hell of fire.

So if you are bringing your gift to the altar,
and there remember
> *that your brother has something against you,*
leave your gift before the altar and go;
first be reconciled to your brother,
then come and offer your gift.
Make friends quickly with your accuser,
> *while you are going with him to court,*
lest your accuser hand you over to the judge,
> *and the judge to the guard,*
> *and you be put in prison;*
truly, I say to you, you will never get out
till you have paid the last penny.

Yeshua's example points out one of the characteristics
of true and appropriate anger.
It was an emotion of the moment.
Emotions are meant to move—either ourselves or another.
When something happens that makes me angry
my anger tries to remove the offending behavior from
my presence.
If you are smoking and that angers me,
an appropriate reaction would be
to inform you it upsets me.
Then you can respond.

But what if I choose to say nothing?
I do not want to bring it up out of embarrassment.

I am ashamed of my reaction,
>or some other reason prevents mentioning it.

What could happen here?
>I can simply forget about it. Unlikely.
>I make a judgment about you based on your smoking.
>Everything I dislike about you will be added.
>Your good qualities will diminish proportionately.
>I may begin to take a real dislike to you
>>and come to judge you a bad person.

A little surge of unexpressed anger can lead to massive
>consequences
>if it is not simply used to express our feeling.

Yeshua illustrates this escalation in his progression
>from holding something against someone
>to damning the other to hell.

Anger not expressed becomes poisonous.
We are about to offer our gift on the altar.
But that hurt against our brother or sister festers inside.
The only help:
>lay aside the gift,
>go,
>make up with the other,
>then return to our religious obligations.

How long we hold on to our anger
>separates the spiritually maturing from the rest of us.

Can we imagine Yeshua
    walking away from the moneychangers
    cursing and ranting about their behavior?
No. He expresses himself adequately
    even overturning their tables.
He has no leftover anger or resentment.
Should he meet them in the future he will not allow the
        previous incident
    to poison his attitude toward them.
He can encounter them at that time in the present.
No resentment. No grudges. A clean slate.
How much better than our usual atmosphere of
        resentment or caution?

To work on our anger means we must first recognize it,
then channel it back to its proper and limited function.
We must learn to befriend it.
It is valuable; it expresses our displeasure.

But to make our anger appropriate
we may need to clean out past resentments
    which render present anger inappropriate.
At the temple Yeshua deals forthrightly with the
        moneychangers.
He does not unconsciously include all the past wrongs
    he has witnessed and suffered.

He does not express anger for past experiences,
>   for all the other incidents which made him angry
>   and now lie buried or "forgotten."
To be angry for more than five minutes
>   is to be angry about past slights and abuses,
>   not the present situation.
Such anger needs healing, not expression.

We must be direct and appropriate with our anger.
Deal with it in the present.
Do not let it fester. Do not hold on to it.
Resolve it as quickly as possible.
We really cannot afford to carry around past burdens.
Resentments are destructive to everyone.
Keep the slate clean.
Reconcile with our friend, if he or she is willing.
>   If not, we have done what we could.
>   Let it go and move on.

Chapter 26

LET GO OF ANXIETY

Fear is a valid, if limited, emotion.
If we are threatened, say by an oncoming truck,
fear is appropriate:
    It gets us out of the way!

But fear today is distorted.
It seeps out in anxiety—
    a diffuse feeling unattached to a specific stimulus
    such as the truck barreling down our side of the freeway.
The pace and force of modern life threatens to over-
        whelm us.
We can be sucked into it
    and suffer a continuous pulse of fear
    invisible like the air we breathe.
Thus we become too anxious, too disquieted for our own
        health
    let alone our spiritual well-being.

Therefore I tell you, do not be anxious about your life,

 what you shall eat or what you shall drink,

 nor about your body, what you shall put on.

Is not life more than food, and the body more than clothing?

Look at the birds of the air:

 they neither sow nor reap nor gather into barns,

 and yet Love feeds them.

Are you not of more value than they?

And which of you by being anxious can add one minute to

   your life span?

If you are unable to do as small a thing as that,

 why are you anxious about the rest?

And why are you anxious about clothing?

Look at the wildflowers, how they grow; they neither toil nor spin;

 but even Solomon in all his glory was not arrayed like one

   of these.

But if Love so clothes the grass of the field,

 alive today and tomorrow thrown into the oven,

will Love not much more clothe you, distrustful children?

So do not be anxious, saying,

 "What shall we eat?" or

 "What shall we drink?" or

 "What shall we wear?"

Ordinary people seek all these; and Love knows you need

   them all.

But seek first Love's Dominion and Love's righteousness,
and all these things shall be yours as well.
Don't be anxious about tomorrow. Tomorrow will take care of
itself.
Let today's own trouble be sufficient for today.

First, practice living in the moment: here and now.
Nothing can be done about the past—it is finished.
Nor about the future—it's not here yet.
But we can engage the present moment, and if we do so,
we will improve both the past and the future.

Meditation is the most common aid in focusing upon the
present moment.
Simple attention to the breath anchors us here and now.
As thoughts and sensations come along, we acknowledge
them
and gently return to the breath.
When we become caught up in things and drift away,
once we are aware we have strayed, we simply return
to the breath.
No need for judgment. No sense of failure.
Drifting is what minds do until trained by meditation.
Drifting is the very essence of meditation.
As we gain experience we catch the drifting sooner,
even in the act of casting off.

Meditation disciplines us to center on the present
even when our meditation time ends.
Even when not meditating, we might try noticing
whenever we find ourselves caught up in past or
future.
This is hard work, so we must cultivate infinite patience.
Not a bad practice, since then we will be able to be
patient with others also.

Such practice helps us move closer to Love's Domain,
where failing or losing are not possibilities.
We have already won all in the arms of Love.
Cherish Yeshua's wonderful images: look at the
wildflowers.
They are weeds, but lovely.
They spring up and flourish under Love's care.
Are we not worth more than they?
Every time we fail, let us immediately pick ourselves up,
with a sense of humor at our mind's innate
stubborness,
and let's return once more to the task.
We have all the time in the world to work on reducing
anxiety
(or other crippling ills).
Whatever small progress we make certainly leavens our life.

Are not two sparrows sold for a penny?

*Yet not one of them will fall to the ground apart from your
       Papa.*

And even the hairs of your head are all counted.

So do not be afraid; you are of more value than many sparrows.

Chapter 27

BE NOT AFRAID

Anxiety and fear are serious stumbling blocks.
The New Testament uses the admonition
  "Do not be afraid" over thirty-five times.

We presume the world a dangerous place.
If we are not careful and cautious we could be hurt.
This may be true for the external world,
  but in Love's Domain fear is not only unnecessary
  but downright harmful.
A harsh parable challenges our fearful attitude
  toward our spiritual life and the risks involved.

A man going on a journey called his servants
  and entrusted his property to them;
  to one he gave five talents,
  to another two,
  to another one, to each according to his ability.
Then he went away.
The one with five talents went at once and traded with them;

and made five talents more.
So also, the one with two talents
made two talents more.
But the one who had received one talent
went and dug in the ground
and hid the master's money.

After a long time the master came back and settled accounts.
The servant with five talents came forward,
bringing five talents more, saying,
"Master, you delivered to me five talents;
here I have made five talents more."
His master said,
"Well done, good and faithful servant;
you have been faithful over a little, I will set you over much;
enter into the joy of your master."
The one with two talents came forward, saying,
"Master, you delivered to me two talents;
here I have made two talents more."
His master said,
"Well done, good and faithful servant;
you have been faithful over a little, I will set you over much;
enter into the joy of your master."
The servant with one talent came forward, saying,
"Master, I knew you to be a hard man,
reaping where you did not sow,
gathering where you did not winnow;

> so I was afraid, and I went and hid your talent in the ground.
> Here you have what is yours."
>
> But his master replied,
>
> > "You wicked and lazy servant!
> > You knew that I reap where I have not sowed,
> > and gather where I have not winnowed?
> > Then you ought to have invested my money with
> >   the bankers,
> > and at my coming I should have received what was my
> >   own with interest.
> > Take the talent from him, and give it to the one with ten."

Identify with the cautious and fearful servant.
Sure, if we are given a lot, we might be confident enough
        to risk it
    as did the first and second servants.
But if we are given only a little, we are liable to be much
        more cautious.
How do I know I won't make a fool of myself?
Won't I be shown up by more talented comrades?
We sit on our assets;
we do not risk developing them for fear of failure or
        embarrassment.

Notice the difference between the parable's world
    and conventional "reality."
Given our experience of life, this is a fairy tale.

No one wins two out of three times.
The parable claims the odds are even higher!
The master implies that the third servant could have
increased his holdings, as well.

The moral is harsh. Yeshua wants to break through our fear.
We are standing on a ledge high up, terrified of jumping
into the safety net.
The teacher pushes us off, knowing we will not get hurt.
He must overpower our fear to rescue us.

No points for caution in Love's Domain. Use it or lose it!

A rich man had a steward:
and charges were brought to him
that the steward was wasting his goods.
So he called him and said, "What is this that I hear about you?
Turn in the account of your stewardship,
for you can no longer be steward."
And the steward said to himself, "What shall I do,
since my master is taking the stewardship away from me?
I am not strong enough to dig, and I am ashamed to beg.
I have decided what to do,
so that people may receive me into their houses
when I am put out of the stewardship."

So, summoning his master's debtors one by one, he said to
the first,

"How much do you owe my master?"
The debtor said, "A hundred measures of oil."
The steward replied, "Take your bill, sit down quickly and
write fifty."
He asked another, "And how much do you owe?"
He said, "A hundred measures of wheat."
The steward replied, "Take your bill, and write eighty."
The master commended the dishonest steward for his
shrewdness;

for the children of this world are more shrewd
in dealing with their own generation
than the children of light.

In this story of immorality,
Yeshua condemns all the pussyfooting timidity and piety
which desiccates much spirituality.
The Way of Yeshua demands everything we have.
Halfhearted efforts avail nothing.
Take a risk, for God's sake!

Our spiritual practice will constantly push us up against
fear and anxiety.
Here a community of disciples proves its value.
We can support one another.

When my own trust is weak, the faith of others can
    support me
  and enable me to take the necessary risks to break
    through.

What a different story if the three servants had consulted
    one another!
The third might find courage to risk his talent in a bank.
He would have ducked the angry outcome.
We cannot make this journey alone.
There is no place for rugged American individuality in
    Love's company.
We are intimately connected one to another
  and we can succeed only through strengthening
  and using that interconnection.
Not only does no one here get out alive;
  no one gets out alone.

Chapter 28

WIN BY LOSING

Happy the poor in spirit:
    theirs is Love's Dominion.

The Way of Yeshua is not concerned with precise
        answers or definitions.
It offers suggestions for dealing creatively with life.
    And it accomplishes this much more successfully
    through intimation than dogma.
Without trying to decipher "poor in spirit,"
        consider some of Yeshua's teachings that might shed
            light upon it
        and hint how we might approach this state of being
        making available Love's Domain here and now.

Yeshua sat down across from the treasury,
        and watched as the crowd gave money.
Many rich people put in large offerings.
A poor widow came and put in two pennies.

Yeshua said,
> *"Look here, this poor widow has put in more than all*
> > *these others.*
> *They contributed from their wealth;*
> > *she from her poverty has put in all she has."*

Not quantity, but attitude, counts.
This is crucial, yet hard to appreciate
> because the world almost exclusively values quantity.
The world may teach that intention counts,
> but only when it does not interfere with results.
We can even import this into our spiritual practice if we
> are not watchful.

Our attitude toward meditation
> is the only significant question from the spiritual
> > viewpoint.
If we meditate to advance along some spiritual stepping
> stones,
> it is useless.
If we meditate to be quiet with God, what's to measure?

> *Who among you would say to your slave*
> *who has just come in from plowing or tending sheep in the field,*
> > *"Come here at once and take your place at the table"?*
> *Would you not rather say to him,*

> *"Prepare dinner for me,*
> *put on your apron and serve me while I eat and drink;*
> *later you may eat and drink"?*
> *Do you thank the slave for doing what was commanded?*
> *So you also, when you have done all that you were ordered to*
> *do, say,*
> *"We are worthless slaves;*
> *we have done only what we ought to have done!"*

This parable illustrates the trouble
    with an ego that has begun to seek spiritual things.
It is tempted to presume itself the master.
It will take credit for everything that goes right
    while blaming what goes wrong on others.

Here's the basic theme of Yeshua's Way:
To succeed, we must lose; to gain life we must let go of it.

> *Whoever would save his life will lose it,*
> *and whoever loses his life for my sake will find it.*
> *For what will it profit you,*
> *if you gain the whole world and lose your life?*
> *Or what shall a person give in return for their life?*

This is hardly the first time we stumble on paradox and
    contradiction.

The last shall be first; the first shall be last.
Give it away or lose it.
Love's Dominion is not our commonly accepted vision of
      reality.
It stands common sense on its head.

We have seen that our sense of ourself, our ego,
     is the crux of our problem in Love's Dominion.
"I" stand in the way of my entering this new way of life.
"I" am my worst enemy on this journey.

Yeshua speaks of "dying to yourself."
But it is not a simple death.
We die for the sake of Love's Domain
     which Yeshua ushers into the world.
His whole life is given over to this mission in the service
     of Love.
So our dying is in the service of Love, in favor of Love.

How might we do this without actually dying?
The musical *Godspell* speaks of
    "putting a pebble in your shoe":
    an apt image for ego training.
We want to find something to put into or take out of our life
     which will cause some conflict, some pain.
Not something so great it is a matter of life and death.

Something small, like a pebble,
    which, nestled in our shoe, will make walking slightly
        difficult.

The real object of this work is not the success of our project.
If I do, my ego will be stronger than ever.
Remember who we are dying for: Love.
    Let Love bring us through.
The secret lies in learning how to let go, to surrender to
        Love, to God.
Only that way lies real progress along the way.

The problems we will encounter will all come from ego,
and it is important to identify its various voices.
Start a real fast as Yeshua did in the wilderness;
    it won't be long before we hear voices too.
But he identifies those voices as "Satan":
    not some little devil, but an image for ego.
Other voices will encourage us to give up.
    "This is too hard!" "What's the use?"
    We'll just relapse into old ways after all this struggle.
    Why prolong the agony?

As we gain confidence and trust in the power of surrender,
we will be able to tackle larger issues, and we'll change
        our life.

We move out of old patterns, ruts of unconscious living,
    and adopt new patterns of consciousness and freedom.

Remember, too, while ego may be the enemy,
on the Way of Yeshua we must love the enemy.
Have compassion upon yourself above all.

We only win by losing.
    It is a hell—
    and a Paradise—
    of an offer.

Chapter 29

CLAIM HEALING

Healing is the physical complement to forgiving sins,
    and it is crucial to Yeshua's ministry.
Do the healing stories, many miraculous,
    come from a pre-scientific age long outgrown?
Shall we pretend they are simply not there?

Today science is beginning to recognize the importance
    of the spiritual dimension in healing.
Chaplains are employed in hospitals,
    not simply as a concession to churches and
        synagogues,
    but because medicine has come to appreciate
    the role of prayer and spirituality in recovery.

The spiritual dimension of healing has been forgotten
    and ignored in our materialistic culture,
    but we need it to promote health and well-being.
Belief in the power of healing

proves a significant component of the healing
    process.
Believe we are going to die,
    and we increase our chances of dropping dead.

While he was saying these things,
suddenly a leader of the synagogue came in and knelt before him,
        saying,
    "My daughter has just died;
    but come and lay your hand on her, and she will live."
Yeshua rose and followed him with his disciples.
Then suddenly a woman
    who had been suffering from hemorrhages for twelve years
    came up behind him and touched the fringe of his cloak,
for she said to herself, "If I only touch his cloak, I will be
        made well."
Yeshua turned, and seeing her, said,
    "Take heart, daughter; your faith has made you well."
Instantly the woman recovered her health.
When Yeshua came to the leader's house
    and saw the flute players and the crowd making a
        commotion,
he said, "Go away; for the girl is not dead; she sleeps."
They laughed at him.
But when the crowd had been put outside,
    he went in and took her by the hand, and the girl got up.
And the news spread throughout the area.

This story is not concerned with healing at all, but with
      raising the dead.
Not even death imposes limits on Love's Sovereignty.

Whenever we experience a deep love we also realize
    this cannot be killed, this is invincible, this is forever.
Our whole Western tradition, Christian or not,
    is a song to the victory of love over death.
In those deaths there is a suspicion,
    a hint, a feeling of triumph over the world.
Are Romeo and Juliet,
      Tristan and Isolde,
    Lancelot and Guinevere defeated by the world?
Only in a certain sense. Their life here is ended.
But the love lives on, certainly in us,
    and we secretly trust, in them as well.
We sense the immortal, the imperishable in Love's depths.

The emphasis upon resurrection in Christianity
    is not imposed from the outside onto Yeshua's
        teaching.
It is there from the beginning.
He raises the dead to life. God raises the dead to life.
God is God of the living, not of the dead.

On our own spiritual journey, Yeshua challenges us
    to investigate our beliefs concerning life and death.

Is death more powerful than Love's Domain?
Is death able to stifle the energy of Love?

For our part, can we trust that Love is able to raise death
        up to life again?
Yes, this goes against the way of the world;
    our culture denies what it cannot see.
Where shall we put our faith?

When something goes wrong,
    are we willing to trust Love to pull us through?
Are we willing to surrender to Love's power?
Are we able to submit to Love's will for us
    trusting that whatever happens is for the best,
    though we may never know how, at least in this lifetime?

Moving to the story within the story,
    we discover a woman willing to risk censure to gain
        healing.

Studies of healing indicate
    that the patient's attitude plays a significant role.
Western medicine tempts us to believe healing is
        something done to us,
    something we submit to, give in to, undergo.
It lulls us into the belief we have no role in healing.

The medicine is all-powerful; our function is minimal.
Science is discovering this is not true.
Our trust in the healing influences the success.
Our ability to claim the healing for ourselves
    allows Love to bestow healing upon us.

When Yeshua turns to see what happened,
    he tells the woman that her faith has made her whole.
No reference to Yeshua's healing power.
The more we consult Yeshua's healing stories,
    the more we see Yeshua is not a healer in himself,
    but rather a conduit for Love's healing power.
That power must be claimed and trusted by the patient
    for healing to happen.
Sadly, Yeshua is unable to heal in his own hometown.
    The people had no faith in him.

But just what do we mean by healing?
It may be helpful to make a distinction between healing
        and cure.
A cure involves total recovery from whatever ails us.
But healing may occur without a cure.
Part of suffering a disease is the isolation and even rejection.

Certain diseases notoriously elicit such behavior.
In Yeshua's day it was leprosy,

today it includes AIDS, cancer, alcoholism, and mental
      illness.
Once diagnosed, the person was excommunicated from
      the community;
this exile might prove worse than the disease itself.
Sick people feel out of it, alienated; the world passes
      them by,
    they no longer count since they no longer contribute
    in ways the world values.
To visit and comfort sick people,
    to assure them they are not thrown out, considered
      useless,
    is to participate in Love's healing power.

To bring hope of recovery,
to share our confidence in Love's healing power,
to pray for them and become vehicles for that healing
      energy
    is often all that is needed for healing—
    even a cure.
Claim this healing ministry from Yeshua. He had no
      hesitation to pass it on.

Yeshua summoned his twelve disciples
    and gave them authority over unclean spirits,
      to cast them out, and to cure every disease and every
        sickness.

212

It is passed to us as well;
professionally, if we practice the healing arts;
to all of us as disciples of Love
     called to bring the good news of Love's healing power
     to those struck down by whatever illness.

A real community of compassion is essential to promote
          healing.
One-on-one healing is almost miraculous,
     and for the most part belongs to Yeshua and gifted
          healers.
But a real community of concern accomplishes miracles
          as well.
It can overcome sickness' isolation and alienation;
it provides an atmosphere of hope and trust in healing;
it offers a healing touch, the physical sensation
     of being included, of being valued,
     of being treasured, that makes true healing possible.

We need first to claim our own healing,
     all the time surrendering to Love's will for us.
But Love also chose us to be healers to all we meet.
Francis of Assisi recognized this;
     terrified of leprosy, he would do anything to avoid
          contact.

Then he realized he could conquer this fear by embracing
      the leper.
The real question: who was healed? Francis, or the leper?

We may embark on the Way of Yeshua for our own health
      and happiness,
   but we quickly learn we are not alone,
   and our well-being is ultimately tied up with the
      health of all.

In Mahayana Buddhism Enlightening Beings take vows
   to seek liberation not for themselves alone, but for all
      who suffer.
In truth, there is no other way.
We are all in this together.

Chapter 30

WHERE TO FROM HERE?

We have examined a part of Yeshua's teachings
     concerning the Way of spiritual growth.
This is not the whole teaching of Yeshua,
     but rather the beginnings of his teachings.
We have not covered practices such as giving away money,
     dealing with envy or lust
     or other things that Yeshua discussed.
Obviously by now we see that work upon any Path
     will occupy the rest of our lives.
There is no point at which we can claim we have arrived.

We can be confident that Love will present us with
          challenges
     as we make our journey which will enable us to keep
          growing
     in confidence and trust in Love's care and concern
          for us.

Be on the alert for ever new opportunities to die to self
    and be raised up in Love.
Seek out chances to be stretched and extended;
    with no chance of failure, what have we to lose?
So, how are we to continue upon our journey?

First of all, continue to study and learn the Path of
    Yeshua.
All his teachings are readily available
    pre-eminently in the Christian gospels,
and perhaps in scriptures not accepted by the churches
    such as the Gospel of Thomas
    or a Course in Miracles.
We will have to sift out what is of Yeshua
    and what may be distortions of his teaching.
Does the scripture accord with what we know concerning
        Yeshua's Path?
    Or does it teach something different?
Does the scripture lead us deeper into the mystery of Love
    or does it suggest something other, such as fear and
        judgment?

Second, we have many writings from Yeshua's friends.
They can widen our appreciation and experience of
        Love's Domain.
We have already met some of these people:
    St. Paul and St. John,

Francis of Assisi and Teresa of Avila,
Thomas Aquinas and Augustine,
Julian of Norwich and Martin Luther King, Jr.,
Teresa of Calcutta and Pope Paul VI,
Don't forget to include his comrades:
Gautama the Buddha, Mohammed the Prophet,
Lao Tsu, Ramakrishna, and others:
the paths are many; the Way is One.

Third, find or found a community.
We have seen the importance of comrades for this work.
We are going against the grain of the world.
Where will we find support and encouragement,
collaboration and challenge?
We are not in this work alone.
This work is for ourselves as well as all.
We cannot be an island cut off from the rest.
Nurture community wherever you may find it.
It isn't necessary that everyone agree on everything.
As Augustine once claimed:

In basics—unity.
In essentials—diversity.
In everything—charity.

217

Paths may differ but, if true, they ultimately do not conflict.

The actual Way is impossible to put into words or thoughts.

Let us learn to live in harmony and communion with those of like minds but different approaches.

Last, keep first things first.

Allow Love's Dominion to nourish and nurture.

Let the love seep in and cast out all false images.

This is a long process. Have patience. Do not give up!

We cannot give what we do not have.

Then remember who this work is ultimately for:

not only ourselves, beloved children of Papa,

but for all the beloved children of Love everywhere.

All are called to this work; few accept.

The harvest awaits and workers are desperately needed.

The task is immense; but as Paul exulted,

With Love on our side, who can ultimately stand against us?

May Augustine's prayer be our own:

Late have I loved you, beauty so ancient and so new,
late have I loved you!

And look, you were within me and I was outside,
    and there I sought you,
    and in my ugliness I plunged into the beauties you
        have made.
You were with me, and I was not with you.
Those outer beauties kept me far from you,
    yet if they had not been in you, they would not
        have existed at all.
You called, you cried out, you shattered my deafness;
    you flashed, you shone, you scattered my blindness:
    you breathed perfume, and I drew in my breath
    and I pant for you:
    I tasted, and I am hungry and thirsty:
    you touched me, and I burned for your peace.